History for Little Pilgrims

Christian Liberty Press
Arlington Heights, Illinois

A publication of
Christian Liberty Press
502 West Euclid Avenue
Arlington Heights, Illinois 60004

McHugh, Michael J. (ed.)
HISTORY FOR LITTLE PILGRIMS
     1. History–Juvenile literature
     2. Social Studies–Juvenile literature

Written and edited by
     Michael J. McHugh
     Edward J. Shewan
     Eric D. Bristley
     Lars R. Johnson
     Kathleen A. Bristley
Designed by
     Eric D. Bristley
Illustrations by
     Vic Lockman

ISBN 1-930092-84-9

Printed in the United States of America

Contents

Preface

Young students need to be given a clear picture of God's providential guidance of history. It is the goal of *History for Little Pilgrims* to provide them with a biblical worldview so that they will see history as "His Story."

Primary grade students often struggle to understand what history is all about. This text will help these students focus on the central theme of history—the building of God's kingdom. They will come to understand this by learning about key figures and events as they relate to this central theme.

Instructors may need to read parts of this book to their students. Slower readers should be encouraged to participate orally in class discussion until their reading skills mature. It is important for instructors to spend time discussing the text, timelines, maps, and pictures with their students. The lessons will be reinforced as the students review the vocabulary words, do the activities, and answer the questions at the end of each unit.

In addition, we encourage instructors to use outside resources to enhance their students' study of history, especially a world atlas and globe. A teacher's manual is available which provides lesson plans and other supplemental activities.

May the Lord Jesus Christ help students gain an appreciation for the work of God in history.

Michael J. McHugh

1 God's Great Story

This book will help you learn about something very important. It is called "history." History is like a story. You may have heard many stories from many books, but the story of history is the greatest one of all. Why is it the greatest story of all? It is the greatest because history is the story about what God has planned. We may call it "His Story." It is not a pretend story; it includes all the true stories ever told. **History** is the story of what really happened long ago. It belongs to God because He works all things together for good.

What is History?

Do you know what history is like? You, for example, have a history—a story about yourself. How old are you? If you are six years old, you were born six years ago. That was the **beginning** of your history.

Do you remember the day you were born? No, but you celebrate your birthday each year to remember your day of birth. Each year you become one year older. Someday your life on earth will be over and then your history on earth will end.

Your family also has a history. To begin with, your parents are much older than you are. They were born before you, so their history is much longer than yours. In the same way, your grand- parents

are much older than you and your parents. They were born many years before you. If you follow the history of your family through the years, how far back might you go? You would go all the way back to when God **created** Adam and Eve in a place called Eden.

History is the story of all the families and people that have ever lived, and you are part of that story. God has given you a special place in "His Story." He chose the time and place of your birth. God will also decide when your story ends.

When History Began

History, however, is much longer than your life. Like your birth, history also had a beginning. It began when God created the heavens and the earth. The Bible tells us that God created all things "In the beginning." What do you think the word "beginning" is talking about? Yes, it is the beginning of time, history, and everything else.

Look at the line of pictures at the bottom of page 4. This is called a timeline. Do you know what the first picture is? It is an hourglass. The sand in the top of the glass takes one hour to slowly drop into the bottom. This shows us when time first began.

Before the beginning there was no time, there were no clocks, there was no history. There was only God. God has no history, because He has no beginning. He was never born. He also has no end.

God is **eternal**. This means He has no beginning or end. This is hard for us to understand because we have a beginning and an end. God created us to live inside time, and God is the Creator of time. That is why history belongs to Him. He is the One who started history, and He is the One who directs it by His wisdom.

ADAM — EVE

GRAN'PA — GRAN'MA

GRAN'PA GRAN'MA

DAD MOM

YOU

Fill in your name and the names of your parents and grandparents.

What is important?

This morning you may have tied your shoes. Is that a part of history? Indeed it is. But it is not a very important part. The Bible, for example, does not tell us about everything that everyone did in Bible times. No, it only tells us those things that are most important to God. Likewise, there are some people, like kings, missionaries, and inventors that did very important things which are written down. In our study of history we will look at those events and people that are important.

The Greatest Story of All

When you eat an apple you soon come to the center where all the seeds are—that is called the core. History also has a core, or middle. It is more than a list of things that happened a long time ago. No, there is a person who is at the heart of God's plans.

Do you know who this person is? He is **Jesus Christ**. He was in the beginning with God because He is the Son of God. Yet Jesus Christ was born as a baby in the middle of history. When He grew up, He did the greatest work in history—He died on the cross to save His people from sin and death. When Christ rose again on the third day, He became the King of kings.

All the stories of history fit together around Him because His life is the greatest story ever told. All the things that happened before He was born look forward to Him. All the things that have happened since He was born look back to Him. The

growth of His kingdom is the center of God's plans. This is why we will look closely at the things God did in building His kingdom.

The End of History

"Tomorrow you will be one day older than you are now. That is your **future**." History is also like that because it has a future. The story of history is not finished today. Many things will happen in your life and the lives of others before it is done. We do not know what will happen tomorrow. But we can be sure of one thing: God is in charge! Nothing catches Him by surprise.

When Jesus Christ returns, He will bring all the stories of history to an end. Then something new will begin. God will make a new heaven and a new earth.

Measuring History

You measure your history by your birthday, or seeing how tall you grow each year. History is also measured by years. A year is the time it takes for the earth to travel around the sun. An event in history is measured by

the year it happened. But there is something important that you should know. All the years before Christ was born are called B.C. (**B**efore **C**hrist). All the years after Christ was born are called A.D. These letters come from two Latin words that mean "in the year of the Lord," for Jesus Christ is still alive. So, if something happened in 100 B.C., it happened 100 years before Christ was born. If in A.D. 100, it happened 100 years after Christ was born.

At the beginning of each chapter you will see a line of pictures at the bottom of the page. It is called a **timeline**. It will help you to see when things happened in history. Learn about the years and the important events that have a picture. They will help you to learn the great story called history.

Little Pilgrims

In this book, you will learn about many things that happened long ago in lands far away. You will find maps to help you learn where they happened. Ask your teacher to show you where these places are on a globe. First find out where you live. Then when you see a new map, find out how far away it is from there.

Some of the stories in this book are found in the Bible. Other stories are found elsewhere. All of them, however, are part of God's great story called history. We will learn stories of people that God used to bring good things into the world. We will also learn about people who

brought bad things into the world. But you should try to learn how God directs all things for His glory.

It is fun to learn about things that took place a long time ago. Our study of history is like a long trip into the past. Do you ever get tired riding in the car on long trips? Sometimes you do, but there are many interesting things to see along the way. As you "travel" through the book, you can pretend that you are a "Little Pilgrim" traveling along the path of history. You will meet many people as you travel. You will learn about their stories. You will learn how they are a part of God's great story.

Don't lose your way! Look for the "Little Pilgrims" along the way. They look like this:

Words to Know

Repeat each of the following words as your teacher says them. Go back in your story to find these words and mark them with a highlighting marker.

history   beginning

created   eternal

future   Jesus Christ

Something to Do

As you travel into the past, how can you remember each place you visited? One way to remember is by drawing pictures. As you move through history, draw each new thing that you learn on a large, white poster board.

Start by drawing a big, long line at the bottom of the poster board. Use a yardstick to make a straight line. On the left end of the poster board, draw an hourglass to show when time began. This is the beginning of history when God created the earth.

In the middle of the poster board, draw a cross and color it red. The red reminds us of Christ's blood when He died on the cross. On the right side of the poster board draw a cloud and color it yellow. This will be the end of history when Christ returns in the clouds of heaven.

Unit 1 Review

After you read each sentence, say the word or words that you think are missing. Write your answers on a separate sheet of paper.

1. The story of what really happened in the past is called _____.

2. You can learn about how history began in the _____.

3. At the center of history is _____ _____.

4. Jesus Christ will return to the earth in the _____.

5. Our study of history is like taking a long _____.

6. You will travel along the path of history as a "Little _____."

ANSWERS: 1. history 2. Bible 3. Jesus Christ 4. future 5. trip 6. Pilgrim

2 The Beginning of History

In the Beginning

God's great story of history began when He made the earth. He made a beautiful world so people would have a place to live. Why else do you think God made the earth? He did not make it only as a place for people to live. He made the earth for His own glory. The Bible says that "God saw everything that he had made, and, behold, it was very good" (Genesis 1:31). God was very happy that He made the world and everything in it.

We should glorify God for His great creation. **Glorify** means to honor and praise God with all our heart. If God made everything for His glory, how should we glorify God? We should glorify Him by praising Him for all the great things He has done. The Bible says we should also glorify Him by loving Him. If we love God, we will obey His commandments. (Read Mark 12:30 and John 14:15.)

0   Creation   The Fall   The Promise

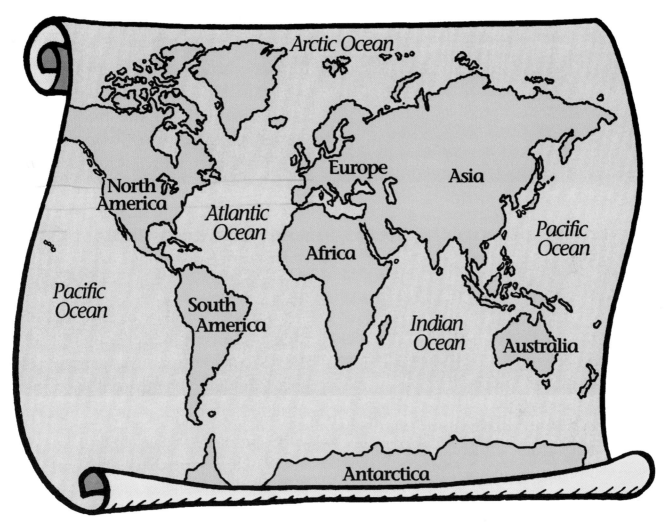

God made our big world with large areas of land and water. The large areas of dry land are called **continents**. The big areas of water are called **oceans**. Look at the map above. Point to the land. Now point to the big areas of water. See if you can learn their names.

Adam and Eve

God created the first man. His name was Adam. God made Adam's body out of the dust of the ground. He also gave him a spirit that will never die. God placed him in a beautiful garden in the land of Eden. God made all kinds of good things for Adam to eat. God also gave Adam

everything that God told them to do.

There was, however, one very important thing that God told Adam *not* to do. God said that Adam could eat the fruit of all the trees in the garden except for one. God said, "... but of the tree of the knowledge of good and evil you shall not eat, for in the day that you eat of it you shall surely die" (Genesis 2:17).

The First Sin

One day, something took place in the garden that made God angry. As Eve was walking in the garden, she heard someone begin speaking to her. When she looked around she saw a snake. Of course, snakes do not usually speak, but Satan spoke to Eve through this snake.

Instead of running away, Eve listened to Satan. He told her a lie. He said she could be like God. All she had to do was eat the fruit of "the tree of the knowledge of good and evil." Eve believed Satan's lie and ate the fruit. Then she gave the fruit to Adam and he ate too.

This sin brought very bad things into the story of history. Do you know what sin is? **Sin** is disobeying

a special job to do. He told Adam to work the garden and take care of it. God told him to give all the animals names too.

God knew, however, that one thing was missing. Adam had no one to help him with all this work. So God made Adam sleep. Then He took one of Adam's ribs and closed him back up. From the rib, God made the first woman. Her name is Eve. Adam and Eve became the first man and wife—the first family. They were happy together because they did

God's rules. Have you ever disobeyed your parents' rules? The Bible says that anyone who disobeys God's rules will surely die.

When you disobey your mom or dad, they are not happy. What happens when you disobey? Yes, your parents will discipline you. In the same way, if we disobey God, He will punish us. The Lord says, "I will punish you according to the fruit of your doings…" (Jeremiah 21:14a).

God's Great Curse

Adam and Eve chose to disobey God. Their sin brought a **curse** on all people. This curse includes all the bad

things that came upon people after Adam and Eve sinned. Thorns, sickness, pain, and death are God's punishment for sin. Because of Adam's sin, everyone has a sinful heart. The Bible says, "For all have sinned and fall short of the glory of God" (Romans 3:23).

After they had disobeyed God, Adam and Eve were no longer happy. The world changed forever. Even plants and animals would now get sick and die. The saddest thing that happened, however, was that God was no longer happy with Adam and Eve.

Since Adam and Eve disobeyed, God made them leave the beautiful Garden of Eden. No longer would they enjoy being close to God in the garden. The first family would now have a hard life, become sick, and someday die.

God's Great Promise

Yet God did not end "His Story" here. Instead He gave a great **promise** to Adam and Eve. He said that a child would be born someday that would crush the head of the serpent! All good things in history would come from this great promise. As you travel through history, you will soon learn about this great promise.

Words to Know

Repeat each of the following words as your teacher says them. Go back in your story to find these words and mark them with a highlighting marker.

history   glorify

continents   oceans

curse   promise

Something to Do

If you have a globe (or a map of the world), point to the place where you live. If you need help, ask your teacher. Now spin the globe. See if you can find the place where you live by yourself.

Ask your teacher to point to the place on the globe or world map where Adam and Eve may have lived. Some Bible students think that the Garden of Eden was in the country of Syria. Do you live far away from where Adam and Eve lived?

If you have a Bible or a story book about the Bible, ask your teacher to read you the stories of creation and Adam and Eve (Genesis 1–3). After you have heard these stories, draw a picture of a beautiful garden filled with animals and flowers.

Unit 2 Review

After you read each sentence, say the word that you think is missing. Write your answers on a separate sheet of paper.

1. History began when the earth was created by _____.

2. The large areas of land are called _____.

3. The big areas of water are called the _____.

4. Adam and Eve lived in the Garden of _____.

5. The sin of Adam and Eve brought God's _____.

6. The Bible says that all have sinned and fall short of God's _____.

ANSWERS: 1. God 2. continents 3. oceans 4. Eden 5. curse 6. glory

3 God Made Many Nations

Two Kinds of People

Though Adam and Eve sinned, God still commanded them to fill the earth. He told them to have lots of children. So Adam and Eve had several sons and daughters. Before long there were many families on the earth. For years, Adam and Eve's family stayed near the land of Eden. The families of their children also lived near each other. Together they built houses, planted crops, and hunted for food.

One day, Adam's son Abel brought a lamb and killed it before God. Abel knew that his sins deserved death.

Adam's other son Cain, however, thought he could be forgiven by trying to be good by himself, and he offered fruit. God accepted Abel's offering and his faith but turned away from Cain and his pride. Cain became very angry with God and killed his brother Abel.

This was the first murder in history. Cain killed his brother because Abel served God by faith. This was the beginning of all the fighting and killing on the earth. Those who thought they were good like Cain have always hated those who trusted in God for salvation, like Abel.

The Big Flood

After many years passed, the people of the earth became even more sinful. They began to do more and more bad things. They became so bad that God said, "I will destroy them with a big flood!" Do you know

The Promise   The Flood   Tower of Babel

14

what a flood is? A **flood** is when water covers dry land. The flood that God sent was so big that it covered all the houses, the trees, and even the mountains.

Only one man and his family did not die in the big flood. Do you know who they were? Yes, God saved Noah and his family. How do you think they were saved? Yes, the Lord told Noah to build a boat. It was called the ark. The **ark** was a very big boat with many rooms. Since Noah trusted in God, he was saved along with his family. Do you know what else God saved?

Yes, God also saved the animals. Do you remember how God saved these animals? God called them two by two, and they came to Noah.

Then Noah took them into the ark. God was very wise in saving all the animals.

After the flood, God put a rainbow high in the sky. A **rainbow** looks like half of a circle; it is filled with beautiful colors—red, orange, yellow, green, blue, deep blue, and purple. Do you know why God gave the rainbow? God made the rainbow to remind us that He will never destroy the earth again with a big flood.

God blessed Noah and his three sons, Shem, Ham, and Japheth, and they lived long on the earth. They were, however, still sinners like Adam and Eve.

After the flood, God gave a new command. He said that if a person murders someone else, that person should be put to death. This was the beginning of policemen and judges. It is called **government**.

The Tower of Babel

After the days of Noah, the people of the earth again forgot about God. They fought with each other and continued to disobey God. The Lord told the people to go and live in all parts of the world. They decided, however, to stay in one place and build a big tower. They thought that this would keep them together and make them strong.

God, however, is the One who directs history by His own plan. As the people were building their tower, God changed their language. **Language** is the sounds and words we make with our mouths. Each

sound has a letter or group of letters. When we put these sounds together they make words.

Instead of all the people speaking the same language, they now spoke different languages. They began to use different sounds and words when they spoke. The people became confused. They no longer understood each other. For this reason, they could not finish building their tower. The confused people had to move away from each other as God had told them to do.

Noah's Three Sons

From the Tower of Babel, the people moved to new parts of the

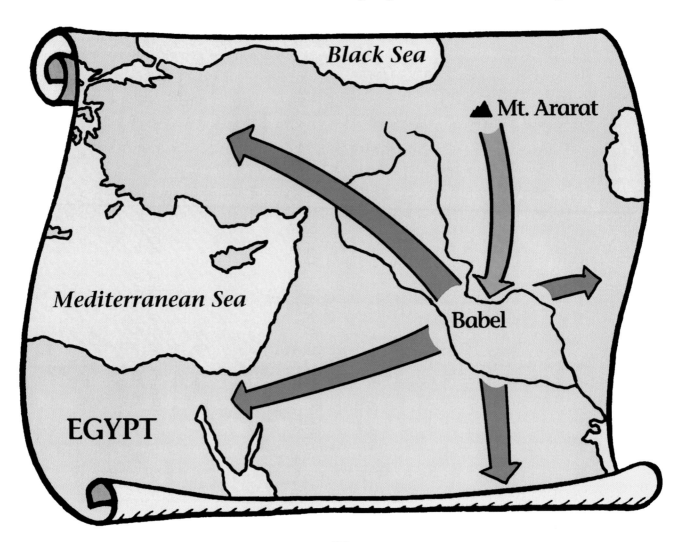

world. They built villages and towns. After many years, these small towns grew into big cities. Then the big cities grew into kingdoms, or nations. A **nation** is a large group of people who live in the same place, speak the same language, and work together. They also are ruled by the same laws.

Laws are the rules that a king or ruler tells the people to obey. In some nations, the laws are made by the people. If Christians live in these nations, they try to make laws that follow the rules in the Bible.

God wanted groups of people to live in separate nations which have their own language. In this way no group of sinners would become too strong and try to rule everyone in the world.

From each of Noah's three sons—Shem, Ham, and Japheth—grew three large groups of people. These people grew into the many nations that filled the earth. Here are a few of these nations. From Shem came the nation called Jordan. It is located in Asia. From Ham came the nation of Egypt. It is located in Africa. From Japheth is the nation called Greece. It is located in Europe.

From Shem came Jordan

From Ham came Egypt

From Japheth came Greece

Words to Know

Repeat each of the following words as your teacher says them. Go back in your story to find these words and mark them with a highlighting marker.

flood	ark
language	nation
laws	government

Something to Do

Noah was a man who loved God. He did what God told him to do. If you have a toy boat and small plastic animals, pretend that you are Noah building the ark. Then help the animals to go into the ark two by two.

Another fun thing to do is to make an animal puppet. Copy or trace the face of your favorite animal on paper. Color it, then cut it out. Now take a small paper lunch bag and glue the face of the animal to the bottom and side of the bag. Write the name of your favorite animal on the front of your paper bag puppet. Put your hand in the open end and you can make the animal "talk."

Unit 3 Review

After you read each sentence, say the word or words that you think are missing. Write your answers on a separate sheet of paper.

1. God saved Noah and his family from the _____.

2. God made the people move away from the _____ ___ _____.

3. A large group of people who live in the same land and speak the same language is a _____.

4. God gave the people at the Tower of Babel many different _____.

5. The rules that a king or ruler tells the people to obey are _____.

ANSWERS: 1. flood 2. Tower of Babel
3. nation 4. languages 5. laws

4 God's Great Promise

After Adam and Eve sinned, God made a great promise to them. A **promise** is when a person says that he will do something. But sometimes people don't keep their promises. God is different than men. When God promises to do something, He does it! God promised to send someone to defeat sin and the devil (Genesis 3:15). Do you know whom God promised to send?

Yes, Jesus Christ was the Promised One. God would send Him to defeat the devil and to set God's people free from sin and death. After the days of Noah, God began to prepare the world for Christ's coming. How do you think He did this? Let's find out.

God's Promise to Abraham

The people who left the Tower of Babel built many cities. One of these cities was called Ur. It was in this city that God spoke to a man named Abram. This city is now in the country of Iraq.

God told Abram to leave his home in Ur and go to a new place, but God did not tell him the name of that country. Although Abram did not know where he was going, he trusted

4000 BC Abraham　　2000 BC Moses　　1000 BC David

God. This means Abram knew God was faithful so he obeyed Him. If God told your family to move to a new place, would you obey?

One night, when Abram was traveling, God promised him that all the families of the earth would be blessed through him. He said that this would happen through a child that would be born in his family line. A **family line** can be traced from father to son. One father has a son, and that son has another son, and that son has another son, and so forth. Do you know your family line?

Abram finally came to the land that God told him about. It was called Canaan, and later on it was called Israel. Though God had given His great promise to Abram, he did not have any children right away.

When Abram was ninety-nine

years old, God changed his name to Abraham. God also promised him that He would give him a son. One year later, God kept His promise and gave Abraham a son named Isaac. This was a great gift!

God, however, asked Abraham to do something that was very hard to do. When Isaac was a little boy, God told Abraham to take him and go to a mountain called Moriah. There God told him to stack a pile of stones and place Isaac on the stones as a sacrifice! (Read Genesis 22:1–19.) A **sacrifice** is an animal that is killed to pay for the sins of the people.

Since God told Abraham that the great promise would come through his family line, how could Abraham sacrifice Isaac, his beloved son? The

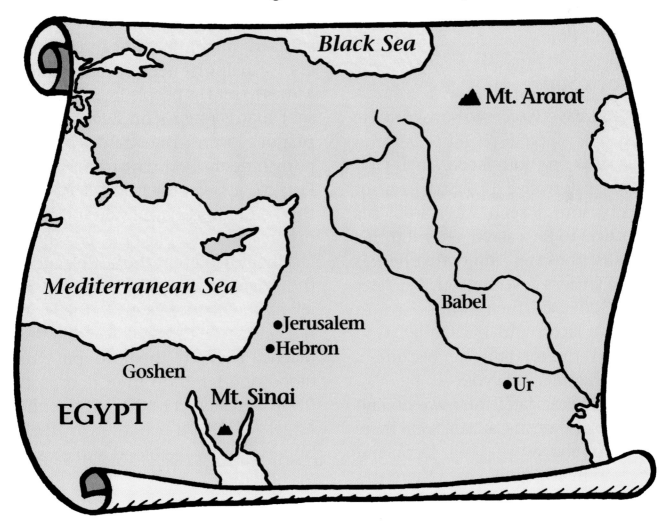

Bible says that, by faith, Abraham believed that God would raise Isaac from the dead! (Read Hebrews 11:17–19.) Because of Abraham's faith, he became the father of everyone who truly trusts in God.

What other person in the Bible does this story remind you of? Many years after Abraham and Isaac had died, God would send His only Son, Jesus Christ. He would give His life as a sacrifice for sin.

Isaac's Sons

God gave Isaac two sons, but He gave his special promise only to Isaac's second son, Jacob. Then God gave Jacob twelve sons. Sadly, one of Jacob's sons, Joseph, was sold by his brothers to be a slave. They did this because they were angry that he was their father's favorite son. Yet later on, God used their sinful ways to protect Jacob and his family. God blessed Joseph and he became a powerful ruler in Egypt.

Many years later, there was no rain for a long time in Canaan. Soon there was no food. So God sent Jacob and his family to Egypt where there was plenty of food. When Jacob's family came to Egypt, Joseph gave them food to eat. You can read about Joseph and his brothers in the Bible (Genesis 37–50). Jacob's sons grew into a mighty nation called the Israelites, and God called them His own people.

The Blood of the Lamb

After Joseph died, the Egyptians made God's people their slaves. They suffered much, but God heard their cry for help. He sent a man named Moses to set His people free. God also sent many plagues on Egypt. These **plagues** were the hard, painful punishments God sent to make the king of Egypt let the Israelites go. But this bad king did not listen to Moses or care about the plagues God sent.

Finally, God sent the last plague—the Angel of Death. He was sent to kill all the firstborn sons in the land. But God saved the Israelites from this plague. He told them to put the blood of a lamb on their doorposts (Read Exodus 11-12). When the Angel of Death came near their homes, he saw the blood and passed over them.

When the firstborn sons of the

24

Egyptians died, then the king finally let God's people go. The blood of the lamb on the doorposts reminds us of Jesus' blood. He would one day die as a sacrifice—the Lamb of God (John 1:29). Only the blood of Christ can pay for our sin.

Moses Receives God's Law

After this, Moses led the Israelites out of Egypt and brought them into the **wilderness**. Do you know what a wilderness is? It is a large desert place. After many days, they came to Mount Sinai.

It was here that God gave the Ten Commandments, or Rules, for His people to obey (Read Exodus 20:1-17). Do you know any of the Ten Commandments? Try to learn all ten of them.

But the people did not obey God's rules. The children of Israel began to serve an idol and to complain against God. Do you know what an idol is? An **idol** is something made out of wood or stone that sinful people worship instead of worshiping God. Because the people turned away from God, He punished them (Read Exodus 32).

After this, God told His people to leave Mount Sinai. He led them to the land He had promised to Abraham. God also gave them a new leader named **Joshua**, which means "God is the Savior" (Read Numbers 27:15–23). Another way of writing this name is Jesus. It was Joshua who brought them into the promised land. This was a wonderful place in which to live, filled with many good things like milk and honey.

King David

As the years passed, the Israelites grew into a great nation. In those days Israel had no king because God was their King. They were ruled by His law. The Israelites, however, became unhappy and asked God to give them a king like the other nations. God was not happy when they asked for an earthly king.

God gave them a king anyway. His name was Saul. When Saul grew older, he did not serve God but followed his own sinful heart. In the end, a people called the Philistines,

who were enemies of God, came and killed Saul.

Then God gave the people of Israel a good king who was born in the town of Bethlehem. He was just a shepherd boy when God called him to become king. Do you know what his name was? Yes, it was David. Do you remember whom David killed with a stone and a slingshot? Yes, he killed a giant named Goliath. King David was different from Saul because David loved God and followed His commandments.

God loved David and gave him His great promise. He said, "...I will set up your seed after you, who will be of your sons; and I will set up his kingdom. He shall build Me a house, and I will set up his throne forever" (1 Chronicles 17:11, 12). God kept His promise, and David's son Solomon built a beautiful house of prayer in the city of Jerusalem called the Temple.

The other part of His great promise, however, was not for Solomon. After very many years

Solomon built the temple in Jerusalem.

Solomon's kingdom fell and the temple was destroyed. God's great promise of a kingdom was not made for any earthly king. It was for the King of kings who was born from David's family line. Do you know who that King is? Yes, it is Jesus Christ and His kingdom will last forever. He is the great King who is now building His church.

Words to Know

Repeat each of the following words as your teacher says them. Go back in your story to find these words and mark them with a highlighting marker.

promise	family line
sacrifice	plague
wilderness	idol

Something to Do

You can pretend that you are an Israelite in Egypt. Take some crayons and color some red on three pieces of paper and tape it to the top and sides of a door in your house. Why do you think the blood was important? (It is an example of Jesus Christ dying for our sins on the cross and God "passing over" us in mercy.)

Unit 4 Review

After you read each sentence, say the word or words that you think are missing. Write your answers on a separate sheet of paper.

1. To defeat sin and the devil, God made a promise to send a Savior, _____ _____.

2. All the families of the earth are blessed through _____.

3. The Israelites were saved because the doorposts were covered with a lamb's _____.

4. The Israelites were led to the promised land by Moses and _____.

5. God promised to set up forever the throne of _____.

ANSWERS: 1. Jesus Christ 2. Abraham 3. blood 4. Joshua 5. David

29

5 God Keeps His Promise

David. It was a miracle when the Son of God became a baby in a manger. A **miracle** is something wonderful that only God can do.

Before this, the Son of God had always lived with God the Father in heaven, but now He had a body like we do. There was, however, one big difference between Him and us. Jesus never sinned! Can you imagine never thinking or saying or doing anything wrong? Jesus was perfect just like that!

When He came to earth, Jesus Christ became the most important person in history. In fact, He is at the center of history! Look at the timeline below. You will see a cross in the middle. God sent the Promised One in the middle of "His Story."

Do you know what an empire is? An **empire** is a big group of nations that has a strong king who rules over them. In the days of the Roman Empire, long after King David, God kept His great promise; He sent His Son into the world as a little baby named Jesus. He was born 2,000 years ago in Bethlehem, the city of

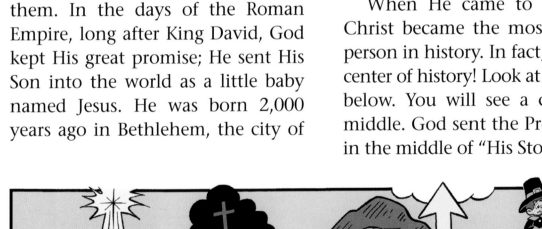

AD 0 Birth of Christ   AD 33 Crucifixion   AD 33 Resurrection

All of God's promises came true in Jesus Christ. Everything that the writers of the Old Testament said about Him really happened. He was the One who defeated Satan. Christ was the One in whom all the nations are blessed, as God had promised Abraham long ago. He also has the same name as *Joshua* (Jesus) who led the Israelites into the promised land. In fact, Christ was born in the family line of King David. This means He would become the great King of God's Kingdom.

Christ began to build His kingdom on the earth 2,000 years ago. Jesus healed many people and told them to turn away from their sins and believe in Himself. Jesus also taught some men to help Him with His work. These men are called **disciples** (students).

Jesus Feeds 5,000

One day, Jesus and His disciples found a large crowd of people near the Sea of Galilee waiting to see Him. He felt sorry for them because they were like a flock of sheep without a shepherd to lead them. So, Jesus began to teach them about the Kingdom of God. He spoke to them all afternoon!

Soon the sun started to go down, and shortly evening would come. The people were so excited to see Jesus, they had forgotten to bring food to eat. They had not planned to stay all day, and now it was time for supper.

Jesus knew that they were tired and hungry, so He asked Philip, "Where shall we buy bread for all these people to eat?" Jesus asked this question to test Philip. Jesus wanted to see if Philip would ask Him to feed the people, but Philip said, "Two hundred coins would not buy enough bread for every one to have even one bite!"

Jesus lived and preached for many years by the Sea of Galilee.

Although the disciples saw Jesus do many miracles, they did not think He could feed such a large crowd. They thought the best thing to do was to send the people away into the nearby villages to buy their own food. After all, the disciples could not feed them and it was getting late.

Then Peter's brother Andrew spoke up, "Here is a boy with five small loaves and two small fish, but how many would this feed among all these people?" Andrew at least had a good idea, but he also did not think Jesus could feed so many with such a small lunch.

Jesus told the disciples to have the people sit down in groups on the grass. Soon all the 5,000 men and their families were sitting down. Do you know what Jesus was going to do next? Yes, Jesus took the five loaves and two fish and began to pray. He thanked God for the food. Then He broke the bread and fish into pieces and gave them to His disciples to give to the people.

The disciples obeyed Jesus. They put the food in baskets and gave it to the people. Everyone ate as much as they wanted and the baskets never became empty! There was so much food left over that the disciples collected twelve baskets of bread. Jesus did not want to waste any food.

The people were so amazed at Jesus' miracle that they decided to make Him king. They were waiting for someone like Jesus to come and set them free from the Romans. Jesus, however, did not come to be an earthly king. He came to be the King over the hearts of men. Everyone who loves and obeys Jesus is part of His kingdom, the Kingdom of God.

Jesus the Savior

Many of the leaders of the Jews did not like what Jesus taught. He told them that they were sinners and needed to change, but they did not want to change. They became so angry, they made plans to kill Jesus.

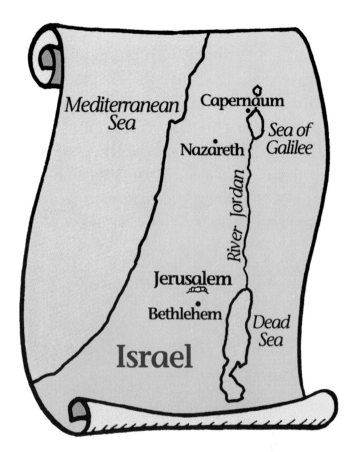

The leaders decided Jesus should die by being nailed to a cross. That was one way criminals were punished for their sins back then. A **criminal** is a person who breaks the law made by the rulers of a nation.

Jesus, however, was not a criminal. He never sinned or did anything wrong in His life. Yet, He was punished like a criminal on a cross.

The death of Christ was not like anyone else's death. His death was to pay for sin. God placed the sins of His people upon Jesus Christ. Instead of God being angry with His people for their sins, God put all His anger on His Son, the Lord Jesus. Jesus was like a lamb in the Old Testament who had to die for the sins of the people.

Jesus paid for *all* the sins of His people on the cross (1 Peter 3:18). To prove He had won the victory over Satan and sin, Jesus rose from the dead on the third day. Do you see how God kept His promise to Adam and Eve? He defeated sin and Satan through Christ. People did not need to sacrifice animals any longer, because Jesus made the perfect sacrifice for sin!

Words to Know

Repeat each of the following words as your teacher says them. Go back in your story to find these words and mark them with a highlighting marker.

empire   miracle

disciples   criminal

The city of Bethlehem

Something to Do

Ask your teacher to read the story of Christ's birth from the Bible. If you have a Bible storybook, your teacher may choose to read from that book about how Jesus Christ was born.

Unit 5 Review

After you read each sentence, say the word or words that you think are missing. Write your answers on a separate sheet of paper.

1. Jesus was born in _____.

2. Jesus is from the family of _____.

3. Jesus fed more than five thousand people with a boy's _____.

4. God's children do not have to be punished for their sins, because Jesus died on the _____.

5. God raised Christ from the dead on the third _____.

6. God defeated the power of sin and Satan through ____ ____.

ANSWERS: 1. Bethlehem 2. David 3. lunch 4. cross 5. day 6. Jesus Christ

35

6 Christ Builds His Church

Jesus Goes to Heaven

After Jesus Christ rose from the dead, He told His disciples to tell the world about Himself. They went out to preach the good news that Jesus died for sin and that everyone who believes in Jesus would be saved.

After teaching them for forty days, Jesus went up to heaven. There He sat down at the right hand of God on a throne. Do you know what He became? Yes, He became the King of kings. God kept His great promise to David. Now Jesus would begin building His kingdom. What do you think His kingdom is? It is all the people who love and obey Him!

Paul the Apostle

Jesus said that He would build His church, and all the power of Satan could not destroy it. So on a special day called **Pentecost**, Christ filled His disciples with the Holy Spirit. The Holy Spirit gave them power to preach God's Word and to build the church. The **church** is the people who believe in Christ and together

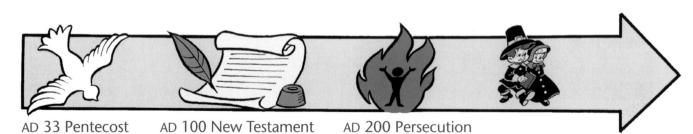

AD 33 Pentecost   AD 100 New Testament   AD 200 Persecution

worship God. Soon the church in Jerusalem grew large as many people trusted in Christ. From there, the good news soon spread to other lands.

It was at this time that God kept His promise to bless all the nations through the family line of Abraham. People from many countries heard God's Word, and wherever people received its good news of salvation churches were started.

Christ used some of His followers to build His church here on the earth. The Apostle Paul was one of them. An **apostle** was a special disciple who was sent by Christ to lead His church. At first, Paul hated the Christians and put many of them in jail.

One day, while on a trip to capture some Christians, Paul was blinded by a great light. Then Jesus spoke to him from heaven and said, "Why are you hurting Me?" Paul was afraid and asked, "Who are You, Lord? What do you want me to do?" Jesus answered, "Go into the city and you will be told what to do."

In a short time, Jesus Christ changed his heart and made him a preacher of the good news. Paul traveled through many cities, preaching wherever he went and starting many churches in other countries. Did you know that the Apostle Paul also wrote many letters to teach the church? The Holy Spirit helped him to write them. Can you find some of them in your Bible?

Christ used the apostles not only to write the New Testament but to build the church. God sent the Apostle Paul to Asia Minor and Greece. He sent other apostles to start

churches in North Africa and Italy. God even sent the Thomas far away to India where a church was begun.

The apostles trained men called elders to carry on their work of preaching the good news and starting churches. An **elder** is a church leader who watches over God's people, teaching them to love and obey God.

In this way God kept His promise of blessing all families on the earth. All the nations of the world are blessed when they hear the gospel of Christ Jesus. He blesses them by sending His Spirit to live in their hearts and to teach them to trust and obey God. Although Jesus is in heaven, He continues to build His kingdom by His Word and His Spirit.

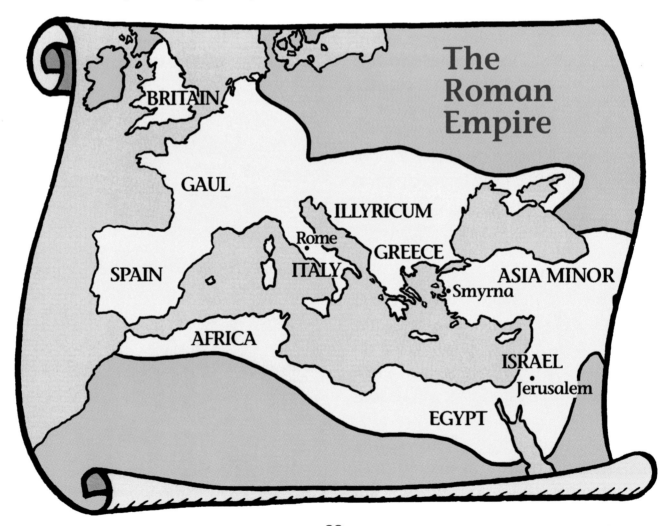

Polycarp the Martyr

About one hundred years after Jesus was born, most of His apostles were no longer alive. They had brought the good news to many places, and many new churches had been started. John, the oldest apostle, wrote about some of these churches in the book of Revelation. He died on the Island of Patmos.

One elder trained by the Apostle John was a man named Polycarp. He became a faithful pastor in the church at Smyrna. Smyrna was a small town in Asia Minor, which you can see on the map on page 38. This church was one of the seven churches that Jesus talked about in the Book of Revelation.

One day, when Polycarp was an

This is an old church in a country called Armenia. Can you find Armenia on a map?

old man, he was arrested and brought before an angry crowd. Some people did not like his preaching. The chief ruler in Smyrna asked Polycarp to turn away from Christ.

In the power of the Holy Spirit he answered, "For eighty-six years I have served Christ and He has never done me wrong. How can I turn away from Him now? He is my King and Savior." Then they burned Polycarp on a pile of wood and Jesus took him home to heaven and gave him "a crown of life." He had become a martyr. A **martyr** is a person who tells people that Jesus is Lord and dies for his faith.

The good news about Jesus was taken by godly men like Polycarp to many places in Asia and Africa. Before long it was preached in Europe. Though many died during these hard times, God's servants never stopped telling people about Jesus—even if they had to die for it.

Christians Suffer

We will now talk a little about the country of Italy. When Jesus was born, Italy was the center of the Roman Empire, and Rome was the main city. This is where many early Christians suffered for their faith.

Powerful kings who ruled the Roman Empire were called **Caesars**. They thought they were like gods and wanted people to worship them. Do you know what worship is?

Worship is when you love someone so much you will do anything for that person. The Bible says that we should worship God, and God alone (Exodus 20:1–6; Matthew 4:10). True worship is when we offer ourselves and our praise to God, glorifying Him above everything else.

The Christians worshiped only the true God and served Jesus Christ. Because of this, the Caesars ordered that many Christians be taken and killed in front of great crowds of

The city of Rome was the place where the Caesars lived.

41

people. Sometimes they fed the Christians to wild lions and other times they were burned on piles of wood. Did they stop telling the story of Jesus? No, the Christians kept following Christ and shared the good news with their neighbors.

As the years passed, more and more people became Christians in the Roman Empire. As many believed in Christ, fewer people followed the old worship of the Caesars. Finally, one Caesar named Constantine became a Christian. He said that the teachings of Christ should be followed everywhere in the empire.

Some Christians were killed in a Coliseum, or stadium, like this one in Tunisia.

Words to Know

Repeat each of the following words as your teacher says them. Go back in your story to find these words and mark them with a highlighting marker.

elder	Pentecost
church	apostle
martyr	Caesars

Something to Do

Many Christians are suffering around the world today! Pray for China, Sudan, and other countries where boys and girls, moms and dads, are hurting and even dying because they love Jesus Christ. Cut out pictures from old *National Geographic* magazines of people and places from these countries. Glue these pictures to a poster board to help you remember to pray for the Christians in those lands.

If you live in a country where people are able to worship God freely, thank Him for the freedom you have. Remember those who suffered and died long ago to give you that freedom.

Unit 6 Review

After you read each sentence, say the word that you think is missing. Write your answers on a separate sheet of paper.

1. Forty days after Jesus rose from the dead, He went up into _____.

2. Christ sent the Holy Spirit to fill His disciples on a special day called _____.

3. One of Christ's followers who built His church was the Apostle _____.

4. A leader in a local church who watches over God's people is called an _____.

5. A man who died for Christ was named _____.

6. The Caesar who said that the teachings of Christ should be followed everywhere in the empire was _____.

ANSWERS: 1. heaven 2. Pentecost 3. Paul
4. elder 5. Polycarp 6. Constantine

7 The Church Spreads

Before Constantine, the church was hated all over the Roman Empire. During his life all this changed. As the good news about Jesus continued to spread, new churches were started and Christ's teachings were accepted almost everywhere. This was good, but a new problem arose. Many people who joined the church did not truly believe in Christ.

Soon many false teachers began to teach things that were not true. These teachers did not love Christ and began to mislead the church. They taught things that were not found in the Bible. So God called men who did love Christ to teach the Bible in the right way. They worked hard to help His followers understand and obey God's Word.

We will learn about three of these great Bible teachers. The first was from Africa. His name was Augustine.

Augustine, the Great Teacher

Augustine was one of the greatest men after the apostles. He grew up in a beautiful city in North Africa. When he was young, however, no one thought that Augustine would ever be of any help to Christ and His church. Although his mother Monica taught him about Jesus, he did not care to live as a Christian.

When he went to school, he became a very good student. Sadly, he also began to live a very sinful life. Augustine did many bad things and followed bad friends. Year after year, however, his mother faithfully prayed that her son would become a Christian.

AD **350** Augustine   AD **400** Patrick   AD **1000** Knights and Castles

One night, Augustine and his friends were looking for trouble. They knew of some pear trees that belonged to a neighbor. Quietly they made their way into the yard and began to shake the trees. They jumped up and grabbed the lower branches and stole all the fruit they could reach. They were so happy that they did such a bad thing, they began to shout and laugh.

As they began to stuff their clothes with green pears, they saw someone coming with a torchlight. They froze in their steps. Then Augustine said, "Everybody run!" So they ran until they were safe. Augustine stopped near his house and tasted the stolen fruit. At once, he spit the pear pieces out of his mouth. "These pears are bitter and hard. Hard as cork!"

Then Augustine asked himself,

The ruins of a Roman city, near where Augustine lived, in modern Tunisia

"Why are stolen things sweeter than things that are not?" He remembered what his mother had taught him from the Bible: "Stolen waters are sweet and bread eaten in secret is pleasant" (Proverbs 9:17). Years later he found the answer to his question; it is called sin. Although the pears were bitter, the sin of stealing was sweet—but only for a short time.

When he was sixteen, his father sent him to Carthage to study. After he had become a school teacher himself, Augustine went to Italy. He was never happy and was always looking for something new to learn. Yet his mother kept praying for her son. Would he ever change?

In Milan, Italy, Augustine went to hear a famous preacher named Ambrose. He was a faithful pastor. Augustine began to listen carefully to what Ambrose was saying in his sermons. One day when Augustine was thinking about how he could find happiness, he picked up his Bible and began to read. Augustine understood that God was speaking to him from the words of the Bible.

Augustine read: "Put on the Lord Jesus Christ, and make no provision for the flesh, to fulfill its lusts" (Romans 13:14). "Putting on" the Lord Jesus Christ means to trust Him to be your Savior and cover your sins. It is just like putting on a coat which covers your body.

At that moment, Augustine became a new person. He turned away from doing bad things and followed Christ. His mother was overjoyed when she heard the news! From that time until the day he died at age seventy-six, Augustine never stopped studying God's Word and teaching it to others.

He sold everything he owned and gave the money to the poor. He also began writing many books. In these books he showed how the false teachers did not follow the Bible. He taught that God is three Persons, called the Trinity, but still one God. The **Trinity** means that the Father, the Son, and the Holy Spirit are one God.

Augustine also taught that everyone is a sinner because Adam sinned in the Garden of Eden. The Bible says, "For all have sinned, and come short of the glory of God" (Romans 3:23). If all have sinned and

Augustine

Patrick

all are dead in their sins, how can anyone be saved? Augustine showed that it is only by the grace of God, by God changing the heart, that a person becomes a child of God (Read John 1:12–13).

Patrick, Preacher to Ireland

Christ's Word spread into one of the nations far from the land of Israel. God used a man named Patrick to bring the good news about Christ to the island nation of Ireland.

Patrick was born in Scotland. When he was sixteen years old, some pirates caught him and took him to Ireland. They sold him as a slave to a chief in northern Ireland. This was not an adventure he wanted! What do you think he did?

Since Patrick was from a Christian home, he cried out to God to help him get out of his trouble. After six years of hard work, he got away from his masters with God's help.

Patrick escaped on a ship that sailed to France. Patrick studied the Bible during this time, and knew that God was calling him to be a missionary. A **missionary** is a person who leaves his country and goes to

An old Irish house made of stone

An old church in Scotland

another land to tell people how they can have their sins forgiven through Jesus.

God wanted Patrick to return to Ireland and preach the good news. The Irish people had treated him badly, but Patrick obeyed God. He was no longer afraid and began to preach in the open fields. Before long, the very chief that had been his master became a follower of Christ! In that place he started the first Irish church. By the time he died, Patrick had started more than 300 churches!

Boniface and the Great Tree

God called another man named Boniface to be a missionary in the dark forests of Germany. He was born in England and became a Bible teacher when he grew up. Forty years later, God led him to preach to the people in Holland, but they refused to listen. Then God sent him to Germany.

He trusted in God who gave him strength to preach to people whose hearts were dark with sin. They were idol worshipers. One day he called together all the people who worshiped the false god Thor—the god of thunder. Boniface told them to meet at the big oak tree. This tree was a special one that the people worshiped in honor of Thor.

Boniface said he would cut down this great tree to prove that Thor was not the true God. He said that only the God of the Bible is the true God. The people stood in fear as he cut it down. The sound of splintering wood echoed throughout the forest, and then there was a tremendous crash! What would Thor do?

Nothing happened, of course! All was quiet! Because of this, many began to trust in Christ and the one true God. Then Boniface took the wood from the tree and built a place where the new church could meet.

When Boniface was an old man, God sent him back to preach the

The gospel spread into Europe.

good news in Holland. One night, when he was teaching some new Christians in the town of Dokkum, a group of evil men made a plan to kill him. The men attacked Boniface with big sticks and he fell to the ground. He died holding copies of the Bible over his head. He was a faithful missionary, was he not?

Lords, Knights, and Castles

During those days, Europe did not have large countries; instead there were many small kingdoms, and each kingdom had a lord. A **lord** was a ruler who owned land and had people working for him called **vassals**. Lords protected their people from pirates who wanted to steal things from them. Many of these pirates were Vikings who came from the nations in the far north. Today these nations are called Norway, Sweden, and Denmark. Can you find them on a map?

The lord would build a castle to protect his people. A **castle** was a group of buildings with thick stone walls around them. Sometimes the lord dug a deep ditch around his castle and filled it with water. If the Vikings came, the people could run and hide inside the castle and be safe. The lord also had special soldiers called **knights** who wore metal suits of armor to protect them in battle.

Words to Know

Repeat each of the following words as your teacher says them. Go back in your story to find these words and mark them with a highlighting marker.

Trinity   missionary

lord   vassals

castle   knights

Something to Do

Wouldn't it be fun to make your own castle? If you have plastic building blocks or *Legos*, you can build a castle with a moat and drawbridge. Sugar cubes can also be used. You can use Popsicle sticks for the drawbridge.

Unit 7 Review

After you read each sentence, say the word that you think is missing. Write your answers on a separate sheet of paper.

1. One of the greatest teachers of the church was _____.

2. Augustine showed from the Bible that everyone is _____.

3. God sent Patrick to Ireland as a _____.

4. Boniface chopped down an oak tree to show that Thor was not the true _____.

5. When Boniface was an old man, God sent him to preach the good news in _____.

6. A place with thick stone walls around it is a _____.

ANSWERS: 1. Augustine 2. sinful
3. missionary 4. God 5. Holland 6. castle

8 Christ Reforms His Church

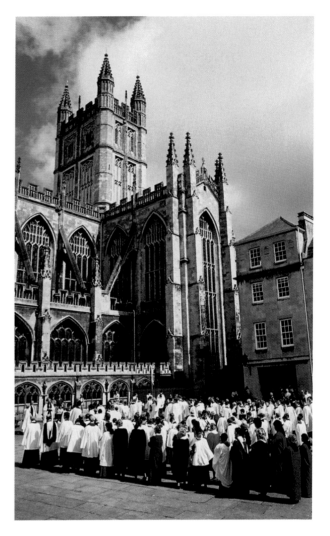

Light in the Darkness

About the year 1500, something took place that changed the world forever. By this time, the Church in the city of Rome had become very powerful and its leaders very wealthy. The leaders of the Roman Church did not tell the people what the Bible says about how to have their sins forgiven. In fact, they did not even want the people to read the Bible themselves! Some men, however, began studying the Bible very carefully. Only the Bible speaks the truth about Christ and His church. In the years that followed, the Bible was given back to Christ's followers. Through the son of a poor miner, Christ chose to change His church.

AD 1517 Luther   AD 1550 Calvin

Young Martin Luther

The miner's son was Martin Luther. His parents loved him very much and taught him the Ten Commandments. Every Sunday they would walk through the narrow streets of Mansfeld, Germany, to go to church. His father was very proud of his son. He had always dreamed of his son becoming a great lawyer, but God had a different plan for Martin's life.

Martin stopped studying law and began to study the Bible. This made his father very angry. All he had planned for his son to be would never take place. But Martin was sure that God wanted him to do this, so he decided to become a priest. Do you know what a priest is? A **priest** is a minister in the Roman Church.

Luther liked to study. In fact, he was such a good learner that he became teacher of the Bible at a new college in the city of Wittenberg, Germany. Luther, however, was unhappy. He always asked himself, "Are my sins *really* forgiven?" He tried to earn his way to heaven through doing good things. He gave up everything he owned and lived in a small room. He swept the floors, cleaned the rooms of other priests, dusted the tables, and wound the clock. Luther was still unhappy!

He also prayed and prayed. He even stopped eating for awhile and became very thin. He would stay up all night to pray and worship. After all this, he still did not find peace with God!

Statue of Luther in Wittenberg

He knew that he could never be good enough to make God love him. He was afraid that God would send him to hell! He knew that **hell** is a very bad place where God forever punishes sinners who do not have their sins forgiven through Jesus.

Saved by Grace through Faith

One day, Luther was sitting in his room studying his Bible. He started to read the book of Romans. Soon his eyes fell upon a verse that would change his life forever. He read, "The just shall live by faith" (Romans 1:17). He stopped and thought about what this verse meant. All of a sudden, the joy of Christ filled his heart! He understood for the first time that it is by faith that people are saved, not by trying to be good. **Faith** means receiving God's free gift of salvation.

This chest was used to collect money to buy salvation. Luther taught that this was against the Bible.

Finally, Luther's heart was filled with peace because his sins were forgiven. He started teaching the Bible in a new way. Then God began to show him how the Roman Church was doing many things that did not agree with the Bible. What really made him angry was a priest named Tetzel who said that if people put money in a special box they could go to heaven faster. Luther wanted to warn the people about these things. He decided to write it down on paper.

When he was done, he had written 95 things that were wrong with the Roman Church!

The next day around noon, he went and nailed the paper to the door of Castle Church. Do you know what day it was? All Saints Day Eve, October 31 (some call it Halloween). The year was 1517. Now many people began to read what Luther thought about the Church of Rome. God planned to use Luther to help the church change.

Martin Luther

Luther's paper was sent all over Germany. A short while later, it had spread throughout Europe! The great leader, or pope, of the Church of Rome did not think it was a serious matter at first. He simply asked his followers to stop Luther from speaking. Luther, however, kept right on teaching the Bible and telling people about the wrong teachings of the Roman Church.

Luther Keeps Preaching

When Luther did not stop preaching, the pope became angry. He commanded Luther to come before him in Rome. Luther knew if he went to Rome the pope would surely have him killed. So he asked his friend, Prince Frederick, to protect him. Since Prince Frederick did not like what the pope was doing, he helped Luther by keeping him safe.

The pope hated what Luther said about the Roman Church, so he ordered the people to burn all of Luther's books. This did not bother Luther too much, though, because in Germany most people kept reading his books.

The pope tried again to stop Luther from teaching the Bible to the people. A big meeting was called for the rulers of Germany, and Luther was invited. This meeting had a funny name—the Diet of Worms ("vohrms"). Luther knew he might be put to death if he went; even so, he decided to go and stand up for Christ and the Bible.

During the meeting, Luther was asked if he would turn away from his faith in Christ and the Bible alone, but he stood strong. He bravely said:

Luther was safe in the Wartburg Castle.

"It is impossible for me to give up what I believe unless I am proved wrong by the Scripture.... Here I stand. God help me. I cannot do otherwise."

The rulers did not know what to do with Luther. So they ordered him to return to his home and stop preaching. They planned to capture him later and put him to death.

Luther's Escape

Luther left late at night by a small gate in the wall of the city. He traveled in a cart for several days, preaching wherever he went. Then his trip led him through the middle of a great forest. Suddenly five men riding horses grabbed Luther, lifted him out of his cart, and rode off with him. Who were these men? Where were they taking him? Was he going to die?

These men took Luther to a big castle in a place called Wartburg. Luther found out that it was his friend, Prince Frederick, who had him captured! He wanted to protect Luther from being killed by his enemies. Frederick's castle stood high on a hill looking over the pretty little town of Eisenach, Germany. Here Luther stayed for almost a year, safe and sound.

While he was hiding in Wartburg Castle, Luther thought about how he could now serve Christ. He came up with a great idea. He thought, "I will translate the Bible into German so the people can read the gospel of Christ for themselves." Luther thought that everyone should read and study the Bible for himself.

As you learn how to read, you will be able to read the Bible—the most important book in the world—for yourself. Thank God that you are learning how to read, so you can read His great book.

Luther translated the Bible into German.

The Church Changes

The teachings of Luther were spread all over Europe and many people began to study the Bible for the first time. They learned from God's Word that the teachings of the Roman Church were very different from what Jesus Christ and the apostles taught.

They learned that Christ was the head of the church—not the pope at Rome. They also learned that doing good things did not help them get into heaven; only by trusting in the Lord Jesus were their sins forgiven. The churches that followed these teachings were called reformed. **Reformed** means to be changed by the Word of God.

Did you ever build a sand castle at the beach? If you build it too near the water, the waves will make the walls fall down. Then you must build the walls all over again in a safer place, right? In the same way, the church was reformed or "built again" by the plan that Christ gave in the Bible.

John Calvin, the French Reformer

The Church of Rome and those who followed it, however, began to hurt and even kill many who followed Christ. But this did not stop the preaching of the Bible or the reform of the church. The men who served Christ in those days were called **reformers**. Besides Luther, a man named John Calvin was one of these important men. He was born in the little town of Noyon, France. When he was older, his father decided to send him to school.

At fourteen years of age, John was sent to Paris to become a priest. He stayed at the house of his Uncle Richard. Though John's stomach often bothered him, he was able to study hard and learn many new things.

As the years passed, John's father changed his mind about his son becoming a priest. He decided he wanted John to become a lawyer. His son obeyed and began to study law in the city of Orléans. He studied so hard that his friends soon called him "Teacher"!

When John was twenty-two, his father died and he moved back to Paris. During this time, he was changed by the gospel and began to follow the teachings of the Reformation. Soon, John Calvin spoke out about his new faith in Christ. Three months later he began to have trouble with city leaders who hated him.

Calvin was in great danger. The police were about to arrest him, but his students helped him escape. Some of them kept the police busy downstairs while others helped Calvin get away through a back window on the second floor.

At the house of a friend, Calvin changed into working clothes and walked out of Paris looking like a poor farmer. He found his way to the nation of Switzerland. There he wrote a book which people still read today. It explains what God's Word teaches and how the Church of Rome did not follow the teachings of Christ in the Bible.

In Switzerland he lived in a city called Geneva. There he taught the people every day from God's Word. He wrote so many books about the Bible that you could fill a whole bookshelf with them!

John Calvin had a special saying: "I offer my heart to thee, Lord, prompt and sincere." This meant that he offered his heart to God right away and with all his might. We should do the same.

Calvin said that God must be first in everything. God is not only first in the church, but also in the nation, at work, in school, and at home. "Seek first the kingdom of God and His righteousness…" (Matthew 6:33). Jesus Christ must be honored as King in all of our lives and in all of the world.

Switzerland is a land filled with high mountains.

John Calvin

God's Word Comes to England and America

God blessed the countries where the church was reformed—in Germany, Switzerland, Holland, Scotland, England, and other places. In England, those who followed the Reformation were called **Puritans** because they tried to purify the Church of England. Charles I, the King of England, treated the Puritans badly. He also sent money to the king of France to fight the French Christians, called the "Huguenots." He even tried to force his ungodly ways on the Church of Scotland.

During the reign of Charles I, something very important happened. By order of the men who make the laws in England, a special meeting was held in London. It was called the Westminster Assembly. It met a long time from 1643 to 1652. The purpose of the meeting was to change the teachings of the Church of England to follow the Bible more closely.

The godly men of England and Scotland who met in Westminster Abbey wrote many important papers. The most important one is called the Westminster Confession of Faith (1647). It includes all the main teachings of the Bible. It is still used by many churches today.

For a short time, the Puritans had freedom to worship God under the rule of Oliver Cromwell, Lord Protector of England. After Cromwell died, though, the Puritans began to suffer again under the rule of other English kings. This is why many of them came to America.

When the Puritans came to America, they continued to follow the teachings of the reformers. God used them to start a new nation—a nation based on the Word of God.

Westminster Abbey

64

Words to Know

Repeat each of the following words as your teacher says them. Go back in your story to find these words and mark them with a highlighting marker.

priest   reformed

faith   reformers

hell   Puritans

Something to Do

In 1456, Johann Gutenberg was the first one to print the Bible. He lived during the time of Luther and Calvin.

If you have a stamp set, pretend that you are the first one to print the Bible. Print Genesis 1:1 or your favorite Bible verse on a piece of paper with your letter stamps. If you do not have a stamp set, you may cut letters out of an old magazine and glue them into place.

Unit 8 Review

After you read each sentence, say the word that you think is missing. Write your answers on a separate sheet of paper.

1. Luther tried to work his way to _____.

2. Luther was changed by this verse in the Bible: "The just shall live by _____."

3. Luther learned that people are not saved by doing good things but by God's _____.

4. The great Bible teacher who lived in Geneva, Switzerland, was John _____.

5. To be changed by the Word of God means to be _____.

6. The people who followed the teachings of the reformers in America were the _____.

ANSWERS: 1. heaven 2. faith 3. grace
4. Calvin 5. reformed 6. Puritans

9 A New World is Found

America is a great land. It is made of two big parts—North and South America. North means the top of the globe and south means the bottom of the globe. Do you live in North or South America?

The First Americans

America is far away from where man was created by God. This is why it took thousands of years before America was explored. The word **explore** means to travel to a new place and learn about the land and the people that live there. Where do people now go when they want to explore new places? People now go to the Arctic, Antarctica, under the ocean, or outer space to explore.

The first people to come and live in America were called Indians. They were called this because the first explorers to America thought that they had reached the land of India. You, however, may simply call them the "first Americans." They were some of the people God sent from the Tower of Babel to fill the earth.

Indians   1492 Columbus   1620 Pilgrims   1700 Colonies

From there, they had traveled north through Asia, east across Siberia to Alaska, and down into the Americas. They came many years before the explorers.

These first Americans were people who lived as hunters and farmers. Most of them lived in small groups called **tribes**. The Indians that lived east of the Rocky Mountains did not build big cities because they liked to travel from place to place. When food was hard to find, they moved.

Some Indians lived in the mountains.

These people, however, did not know Christ. They worshiped spirits that they thought lived in trees, hills, and the sky. **Worship** means to serve someone or something with all your heart. These first Americans worshiped these spirits because no one told them about the true God—the God of the Bible.

For many years, only the American Indians lived in North America. But about A.D. 1000, brave explorers from Norway and Denmark crossed the ocean and visited America. These explorers were called Vikings. They knew much about sailing boats. They sailed their small boats first to Iceland and Greenland, and then to North America. Can you find the way that they traveled on the map on page 68?

Columbus finds the New World

In the year 1492, an explorer named Christopher Columbus sailed the ocean blue from Spain to America. Columbus made four trips to this new world. He also showed others how to get across the wide ocean to the New World. Soon many explorers sailed there. Explorers from Spain traveled over all America, especially South America.

The first city to be built by Europeans in North America was called Saint Augustine. It was named after the great Bible teacher we learned about earlier. Saint Augustine was built on land that is now part of the state of Florida. Can you find it on the map?

The Pilgrims Come to America

England and Holland sent explorers to North America, too. Soon people from their countries wanted to live in America. Many of the people who sailed to North America followed the teachings of the reformers and tried to live by the Bible.

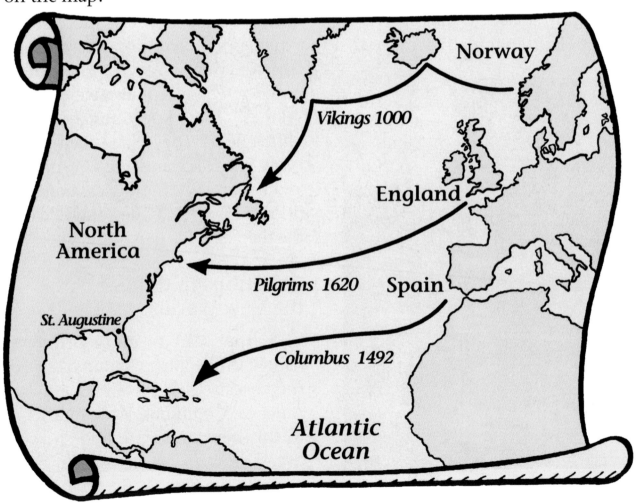

A special group of Christians from England, called **Pilgrims**, came to America so they could worship God freely. They were Christians who had suffered much for following Christ and left England to start a new life.

In the year 1620, a brave group of Pilgrims sailed from England to the New World in their ship called the *Mayflower.* After their long trip, they left their ship and set foot on a beautiful new land. This was now their new home. They called their first home Plymouth Colony.

A model of the *Mayflower*

The Pilgrims lived at peace with the Indians who lived around them. These first Americans even joined them in a big meal to thank God for His blessings. Many Americans still remember that day by eating a special meal on "Thanksgiving Day" each November.

The American Colonies

As the years passed, many other people came from Europe. The King of England said that most of the land of North America belonged to England. Soon England had many colonies in North America. A **colony** is a place that is ruled by a faraway country. The Pilgrims and Puritans lived in what was called New England. It is still called that today.

One hundred years later, however, the people did not serve God like the first Pilgrims did. Many of them had

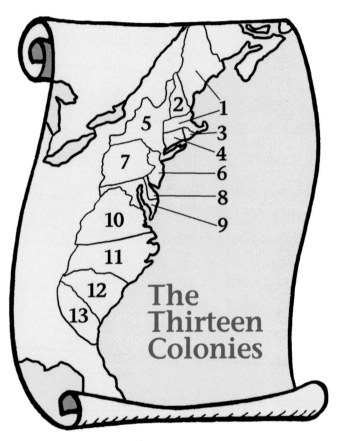

The Thirteen Colonies

1. Massachusetts
2. New Hampshire
3. Rhode Island
4. Connecticut
5. New York
6. New Jersey
7. Pennsylvania
8. Delaware
9. Maryland
10. Virginia
11. N. Carolina
12. S. Carolina
13. Georgia

wandered away from Christ. The American people had forgotten how their parents and grandparents had suffered for following Christ. After all, that had happened many years ago. What did that have to do with them? Besides, they were busy working and making money. They thought they did not have time for serving Christ.

Jonathan Edwards, the Great Preacher

Jonathan Edwards was a famous preacher during a time called the "Great Awakening." Do you know what an awakening is? Awakening is when you wake up in the morning. You feel fresh and strong. You feel like a new person.

The **Great Awakening** was a time when people woke up, not from sleep, but from sin in their hearts. God awakened their sleepy hearts to faith in Christ. Now they understood the good news of Christ's death and received eternal life.

God used a man named Jonathan Edwards to wake up the people. He preached like the reformers. God used Edwards and others to lead the American people back to His Word.

Jonathan Edwards

When he was a young boy, Jonathan went to a small church. He would also go to the woods near his house for times of prayer. Years later when he went to college, however, he forgot about God and His Word and spent most of his time just studying what men without Christ taught.

Then he began again to look for God. He felt sad because he did things that did not please God. He wanted to know how to be saved. God woke him from the sleep of sin and gave him new life!

After God saved Jonathan Edwards, he wanted to serve God by preaching the good news about Christ. He told the people that a person is saved not by trying to be good, but by being born again by the Holy Spirit. This was the same thing that Martin Luther preached 200 years before. The American people also needed to hear the same words.

People from all over the American colonies came to hear him preach. God used these visitors to take the good news back to their cities. This was how the Great Awakening spread to other parts of North America.

God was making the American people ready for something new. Do you know what that was? They were about to start a new nation. He wanted them to build a nation that was based on faith in the Word of God.

Do you too want to come to Jesus? You certainly may come to Him, too. He wants you to say, "I am sorry for

The churches in America were made strong by the Great Awakening.

all the bad things I say and do. Please forgive me. I believe that Jesus died on the cross for me. He was punished for my sins. I also believe that he rose again on the third day. Please come into my heart."

Words to Know

Repeat each of the following words as your teacher says them. Go back in your story to find these words and mark them with a highlighting marker.

explore	tribes
worship	Pilgrims
colony	Great Awakening

Something to do

The Pilgrims and the Indians thanked God for giving them food to eat. Do you thank God for the food you eat? Before every meal you should thank the Lord for all the good things He gives you to eat.

Unit 9 Review

After you read each sentence, say the word that you think is missing. Write your answers on a separate sheet of paper.

1. The first Americans were called _____.

2. The men who came from Norway and Denmark to North America were called _____.

3. In 1492, America was rediscovered by _____.

4. To thank God for His blessings, a thanksgiving feast was enjoyed by the Indians and the _____.

5. The thirteen colonies were located in North _____.

6. A great preacher during the Great Awakening was Jonathan _____.

ANSWERS: 1. Indians 2. Vikings
3. Columbus 4. Pilgrims 5. America
6. Edwards

10 Freedom for a New Nation

Williamsburg, Virginia, was the capital of the colony of Virginia.

Life was not easy in the colonies. The king of England made it hard and these colonists suffered much. That is why they wanted freedom to rule themselves. God was with them and showed them the way to go.

King George of England made laws that hurt the American people. He wanted the colonists to pay him more and more money. Finally they sent a letter to the king. They asked him to change the bad laws. Instead of listening to them, the king sent soldiers to make sure they paid him money.

England Rules   1776 War for Independence   1787 U.S. Constitution

Windsor Castle is the place where the kings and queens of England sometimes live.

Patrick Henry, Lover of Freedom

There was a great American who loved freedom. His name was Patrick Henry. He spoke to the leaders of the colony of Virginia. He said, "The king has no right to take any more money unless the men of Virginia agree with the king's plan."

The king of England did not want the American colonies to be free. Patrick Henry saw what was about to happen. He warned the men of Virginia that war was coming soon. He said: "I know not what path others may take; but as for me, give me liberty, or give me death!"

75

The colonists became angry. They decided to meet in the city of Philadelphia and make a plan. What do you think they decided to do? They planned to fight for freedom!

George Washington, Freedom Fighter

On July 4, 1776, the colonial leaders signed a paper called the **Declaration of Independence**. This paper said the American people were free from the rule of England.

This meant that there would be a war, because King George of England wanted to keep them under his rule.

The colonists needed someone to lead them against King George. They chose a man named George Washington. Now the two Georges would fight each other!

England sent soldiers with guns, food, and supplies. The poor farmers who joined General Washington's army did not have much compared to King George's men. They loved freedom, however, and wanted to fight for it.

The colonists fought hard and some died. Other soldiers became very sick. During the long winters, they also became hungry and cold, but they kept on fighting for freedom! General George Washington helped his men to keep on fighting. Then things began to change.

At the Battle of Yorktown, the colonists finally beat the English. At last the war was over. The old English colonies were now a new free nation called the United States of America.

America's First President

After the war, Washington led a group of men that met to write a plan for the new nation. They met in Philadelphia. What kind of nation would it be? After they talked and argued and prayed, they finally wrote a plan called the Constitution. The **Constitution** is a paper that tells the most important laws in the land which everyone must obey. The people did not want a king to rule their new country. They wanted the law to rule their new nation. Because the people followed the Lord, God gave them a good plan. It has helped

British soldiers were called redcoats.

George Washington's home, Mt. Vernon, is in Virginia.

to keep the people of the United States free for many years.

One of the laws said that the people should choose someone to lead their country every four years. Who do you think they chose? Yes, George Washington was chosen to be the first president of the United States. A **president** is the leader of a country, but he is not a king. He can only do what the law says.

President Washington was an honest and godly leader. He encouraged the American people to pray and follow the Holy Bible.

Jefferson was one of these leaders. He worked hard to free America from the rule of King George of England.

Jefferson was born in Virginia. He had helped to write the paper called the Declaration of Independence. Twenty-five years after the United States became a nation, Thomas Jefferson became its third president. He thought, however, that he was wiser than God. One time, he took a Bible and cut out all the parts that he did not like, all the parts that talk about the great miracles done by God's hand.

Thomas Jefferson

Not everyone in America that helped to start the United States believed in Christ. They did, however, love freedom. They wanted freedom to follow their own hearts. T h o m a s

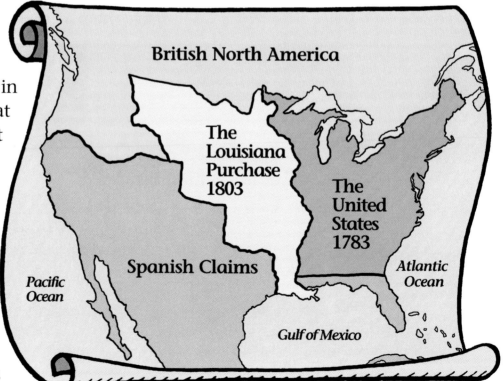

British North America

The Louisiana Purchase 1803

The United States 1783

Spanish Claims

Pacific Ocean

Atlantic Ocean

Gulf of Mexico

President Jefferson did many important things while he was president. He bought a large piece of land called the Louisiana Territory. This land was bought from France and made the United States bigger than it was before. How much bigger did it become? Look at the map.

Words to Know

Repeat each of the following words as your teacher says them. Go back in your story to find these words and mark them with a highlighting marker.

Declaration of Independence

Constitution

president

Something to Do

"My Country 'Tis of Thee" is a beautiful song that tells about our great land and the freedom that we enjoy. Sing this song with all your heart. Let people know that you love this great nation in which you live.

Unit 10 Review

After you read each sentence, say the word that you think is missing. Write your answers on a separate sheet of paper.

1. A great American who loved freedom was Patrick _____.

2. The leader who led the American army against the English was George _____.

3. The colonists signed the Declaration of Independence on July 4, _____.

4. The colonists finally beat the English in the Battle of _____.

5. Washington joined a group of men to write a new plan for the nation called the _____.

6. Washington was chosen by the people to be the first _____.

7. A large piece of land called the Louisiana Territory was bought from France by President _____.

ANSWERS: 1. Henry 2. Washington
3. 1776 4. Yorktown 5. Constitution
6. president 7. Jefferson

11 America Moves West

Lewis and Clark Explore the West

When Meriwether Lewis was ten years old, his family moved from Virginia to upper Georgia. Meriwether had wonderful times as he grew up on a big farm which was called a **plantation**. He spent most of his time outside in God's beautiful creation. He enjoyed learning how to hunt. He also learned about all kinds of plants and animals that were in the forest. Meriwether Lewis also enjoyed learning new things at school.

One day in school, his teacher said that the earth spins around like a top. Do you have a top that spins? That is how the earth spins. Meriwether was so excited that he started to jump high in the air, hoping to see the earth move under his feet—but nothing happened! Meriwether was sad. Then his teacher told him that he was moving with the earth so he could not see the earth spinning. This boy loved to learn new things.

Meriwether's step-father died when he was eighteen years old, so he decided to move back to Virginia

A plantation house in Virginia

1804 Lewis and Clark   1850 Travel West   1900

with his mother, brothers, and sister. He felt it was his duty to care for his family and "Locust Hill" plantation. Meriwether also made sure that his brothers and sister went to school just as he had done.

When Lewis was twenty, he joined the army. After Lewis served his country for five years, President Jefferson asked him to be his private secretary. Lewis accepted the job right away and moved into the White House with the President. Lewis took care of all the President's meetings.

President Jefferson had a dream of finding an easy way to travel up the Missouri River all the way west to the Pacific Ocean. He asked his friend Meriwether Lewis to find the way. Lewis agreed to go because he wanted to serve his country and he loved adventure. In 1803, Lewis asked a

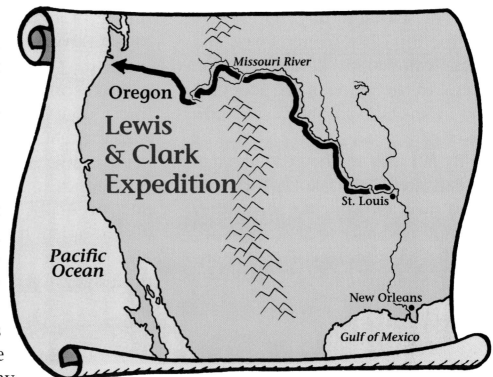

man named William Clark to join him on the big trip.

William Clark was a good man to go on this trip because he had served in the army for many years. He helped make the frontier safe for American settlers who had moved west. Clark had fought the Indians and helped General Wayne defeat them in the Battle of Fallen Timbers. Clark and Lewis had been soldiers together.

Clark wanted to serve his country very much, so he told Lewis he would go on this big trip west. Right away he started getting things ready for the trip. That winter, Lewis and Clark camped in Illinois near St. Louis. In the spring of 1804 they set out in several boats up the Missouri River.

By fall they reached the Mandan Indians in North Dakota. They sent extra men and supplies which they did not need back to St. Louis. They decided to spend the winter at the Mandan camp and leave early in the spring of 1805 to travel up the Missouri to its beginning. By God's grace, they found an Indian **guide** named Sacagawea who helped them find their way through the wilderness. She also asked her people to help the explorers on the way.

The Indians gave them horses to ride over the mountains to the beginning of the Columbia River. This river took them all the way to the Pacific Ocean. They spent the

winter near the mouth of the Columbia River. They wanted to travel back home by sea but no ship ever came. The next spring they returned the way they had come.

They reached St. Louis on September 23, 1806. Everyone was excited that they returned safely. Since no one had heard from them for a year and a half, people thought they were lost. Together Lewis and Clark had found a way to reach the Pacific Ocean by traveling up the Missouri River, crossing over the mountains, and moving down the Columbia River. The President and the people were proud of what Lewis and Clark had done.

Wagon Trains and Pioneers

The United States has changed a great deal over the years. When it was just beginning, people would travel into new parts of North America with a horse and wagon.

Often, families would travel together in large groups of wagons called **wagon trains**. People who lived in the eastern part of North America would go west in wagons searching for new land so they could build a nice home and raise crops or animals. The early families who traveled west were called **pioneers**.

Pioneer families usually lived in log **cabins** that they made from trees they chopped down. The fathers hunted for food in the forest so their families would have meat to eat. Can you imagine eating a delicious supper of deer or rabbit or even bear meat?

Life was not easy for the early pioneers. They had to work hard to grow food and were often lonely. These people often had to fight with Indians who did not like strangers coming into their land. Still, many of the early pioneers often enjoyed a good life when they built churches and followed the teaching of God's Word.

Little by little, the western part of North America began to fill up with new settlers. **Settlers** are people who come to a new part of the country to start farms and towns. As time went by, more of the lands in the western territory were added to the United States. This country started with only thirteen states, but grew into a big country of fifty states!

Words to Know

Repeat each of the following words as your teacher says them. Go back in your story to find these words and mark them with a highlighting marker.

guide	plantation
cabins	wagon train
settlers	pioneers

Something to Do

If you have a craft store nearby, your parents might be able to buy a small kit that will let you build your own covered wagon, log cabin, etc. Home school fairs often have craft supplies and kits as well.

Your teacher may help you make these things with items found around the house. For example, you could use an old shoe box for a covered wagon. For the cover, take a blank sheet of paper and glue each end of the paper to opposite sides of the box. Cut circles for wheels out of poster board, then color and glue them to your wagon.

Unit 11 Review

After you read each sentence, say the word that you think is missing. Write your answers on a separate sheet of paper.

1. The famous explorer who discovered a way to the Pacific Ocean was Meriwether _____.

2. President Jefferson wanted to find a way to the Pacific Ocean by following the _____ River.

3. Jefferson told Lewis to take someone else on the big trip and he chose William _____.

4. Early Americans traveled west in groups called _____ _____.

5. Those who traveled west in wagons in search of new lands were called _____.

6. People who come to a new part of the country and start farms and towns are called _____.

ANSWERS: 1. Lewis 2. Missouri 3. Clark 4. wagon trains 5. pioneers 6. settlers

12 The Nation Grows

Noah Webster's Big Dictionary

Noah Webster was still in school during the war for America's freedom. After he finished college, Webster began to teach in a small country school. Schools during this time had very few books. Often, a whole room full of students would have to share one or two books. This made teachers like Noah Webster very sad.

Webster decided to write a new school book just for American students. He called his book *The American Spelling Book*. Soon, millions of children throughout the United States were studying from this new book. Noah Webster was happy that children in America finally had a school book that was written just for them.

When Noah Webster was fifty years old, he began the most important job of his life. He put together the first American dictionary. Have you ever looked carefully at a **dictionary**? It is a big

1800 Webster   1861 Civil War   1880 D.L. Moody

book that tells what words mean. Because Webster was a Christian, he took many of the meanings of words from the Bible.

Robert E. Lee and the War Between the States

Do you remember how many states were part of the United States in the beginning? That's right, thirteen. By 1860, the United States had grown to include thirty-three states. Some of the new states were very far away from each other. California was way out

west and Minnesota was way up north. As the United States grew, many problems began to develop between the states.

Many leaders in the South were upset with laws passed in the capital city of Washington, D.C. They thought these laws took power away from the states. The leaders in the North, though, believed it was wrong for Southerners to own people as **slaves**. So the leaders in many states became angry with each other.

After Abraham Lincoln was elected president in November

1860, several of the Southern states decided to leave the United States and start a new nation. They called it the Confederate States of America. This began the **War Between the States**, a very sad time in the story of our country.

Robert E. Lee had been an important officer in the United States army for many years. He was sad when he heard that his home state, Virginia, was leaving the United States to join a new nation. The people in the North were going to fight the people in the South to keep them from starting their own country. Mr. Lee had to decide on which side he would fight.

Although Lee loved his country, he loved Virginia even more, so he decided to join the South in its war for freedom. Robert E. Lee became a very important general in the army of the South.

Thousands of young men died in the war between the North and South. This war lasted four long years. General Lee and his men fought hard and well, but in the end, the Southern army lost the war. The Union was saved and soon the slaves were set free.

Young Dwight L. Moody

During the War Between the States, the country needed to hear the Word of God. God called a young shoe salesman to tell the people of America the good news of Jesus Christ. That man was Dwight L. Moody.

Dwight was born in 1837 in Massachusetts. When he was four years old, his father died. Dwight never forgot it. Now his mother had to take care of her seven children all by herself. Though the family faced many hard times, Dwight always found time for a little fun.

At the end of school one year, the teacher asked Dwight to recite a poem. So he brought a box and set it on a table in front of the class and began to speak. By the time he finished, everyone was crying because his words were so sad. Then he opened the box and, all of a sudden, out jumped a tomcat! "Scat!" cried Dwight. The screams and laughter that followed were great. Dwight always liked a good laugh.

When he was seventeen, Dwight left home and went to Boston. He asked his uncles if he could work for them in their shoe store. They said he could if he promised to go to church every Sunday. He agreed and started going to church. His Sunday school teacher taught him from the Bible. He taught him that Jesus died on the cross for the sins of His people. Right away, Dwight believed God's great promise and was saved.

Dwight L. Moody preaching

89

Mr. Moody, the Evangelist

Not long after this, Moody decided to move west to the big city of Chicago and started inviting his friends to church. He also organized a Sunday school, but he still had a job selling shoes. All the time he was selling shoes, he kept thinking about the children in his Sunday school. Then Moody made the hardest choice in his life. He quit his job and became a missionary to the children of Chicago.

During the War Between the States, Moody told the young soldiers about Christ. He became a mighty preacher and spoke the good news about Christ not only in Chicago but also in Scotland, Ireland, England, and Wales. Can you find these countries on a globe?

Then he saw that other people had to learn how to spread the good news. So he began a school in Chicago that is now called the Moody Bible Institute. Students are still trained there to take the Word of God to people around the world.

Have you ever gone to a fair? Fairs have many things to look at and lots

The city of Chicago is near Lake Michigan.

90

of fun things to do. Mr. Moody preached at a fair once, but this fair was really big. It was called a World's Fair. Millions of people came to it and many of them heard the good news of Jesus Christ from Mr. Moody.

He kept on preaching for many years till one day, three days before Christmas, God called him home to heaven. America was very blessed to have a preacher like Mr. Moody. He did so much to help our country.

Words to Know

Repeat each of the following words as your teacher says them. Go back in your story to find these words and mark them with a highlighting marker.

slaves   dictionary
War Between the States

Something to Do

Make your own spelling book just like Noah Webster did. Ask your teacher to take a sheet of lined paper and fold it in half. Fold it in half again; then fold it in half one more time. Cut the paper on each fold line. You will have eight pieces of paper.

Take your phonics book or reader and write down all your favorite words on the eight pieces of paper. When you are done, ask your teacher to staple the pieces of paper together. Now you have your own spelling book and can memorize how to spell those words!

Unit 12 Review

After you read each sentence, say the word that you think is missing. Write your answers on a separate sheet of paper.

1. Noah Webster put together the first American _____.

2. In America, by the year 1860, there were thirty-three _____.

3. An important leader in the Southern army was General Robert E. _____.

4. General Lee loved his country but he loved more his home state of _____.

5. To tell America the good news of Christ, God called a young shoe salesman named Dwight L. _____.

ANSWERS: 1. dictionary 2. states 3. Lee 4. Virginia 5. Moody

13 A Nation Grows Strong

George Washington Carver Studies Plants

In 1864, another great American by the name of George Washington Carver was born. This child was born to parents who were black slaves in the state of Missouri. Can you find this state on a map? Sadly, both of George's parents were taken away from him during the War Between the States. He grew up in the home of friendly neighbors who loved him very much.

George W. Carver   Thomas A. Edison   Theodore Roosevelt

As George grew up, he began to learn about how plants grow. He liked to explore in the woods and study plants. His new parents taught him how to read so he could learn about God's creation. George loved to read and work hard.

George decided to go to school so he could learn more about how things grow. He wanted to be useful to God and to others. After George finished college, he began to teach his students how to grow food. Carver also helped many farmers and taught them about plants.

One of the plants that Carver taught the farmers about was the sweet potato. Another one was the peanut plant. Do you know what comes from the peanut plant? Yes, peanut butter. Children everywhere love to spread peanut butter and jelly on bread and eat it. Carver found many other ways to use peanuts too.

Since Carver was such a good teacher, American farmers began to grow more and more food. God blessed the United States through Carver, because the farmers had so much food that they sold it to other countries around the world. Today, American farmers continue to grow so much food that they often sell it to people in other lands.

Sweet potatoes

Peanuts

Thomas Edison Invents New Things

God also blessed America through Thomas Edison. Like many young boys, he loved to make things. He set up a workshop in his home. Thomas helped his mother fix many things around the house. He also made special things for his sister.

Although he worked hard, Thomas did not do well in school. His teachers thought that he was not able to learn. He was always thinking about other things and forgetting to do his school work. So Thomas' mother took him out

of school. She decided to teach her son at home.

Thomas liked to learn at home. He also enjoyed making new things that helped others. When he was twelve, Thomas went to work as a newspaper boy at the local train station. Thomas sold newspapers and candy to people riding the train so he could buy books. The books helped Thomas learn even more things.

As Edison grew older, he saved his money so he could start his own business. This way he could spend all of his time making things that would help others.

After years of hard work, Edison made many new inventions such as the electric light bulb, the phonograph, and the movie camera. Do you know what an **invention** is? It is a new tool or machine that someone thinks about in his mind; then he draws it on a piece of paper and then builds it. Can you think of other inventions?

The many new inventions that Thomas Edison made changed the way people in the United States lived. Before Edison made the electric light bulb, all homes were lit by candles or oil-burning lamps. Close your eyes and think what it would be like in your home if there were no electric lights. How would you see at night?

Thomas Edison also helped to make the telephone better. Many people throughout the world think that Edison was the best **inventor** the world has ever known. Stop and thank God for giving Thomas Edison a good mind and a desire to work hard to serve other people. Maybe you can work hard and invent useful things someday like Edison did.

New Ways to Travel, Work, and Live

The United States has changed much over the years. It was hard to travel in pioneer times when people used wagons, trains, and even hot air balloons. We now have fast cars and airplanes to take us from place to place. You can fly across the country in a few hours today—a lot faster than bumping along in a wagon for two or three months!

There are many new ways of doing things besides the ones discovered by Carver and Edison. We go to the supermarket now to buy most of our food instead of growing it all ourselves. Besides learning from

books, we can now use computers. We should thank God for the many inventions and discoveries that help us to live better and work faster.

Theodore Roosevelt, the Great Outdoorsman

Theodore Roosevelt was a very sick boy during the War Between the States. His nickname was Teddy. He spent a good deal of time at home trying to get better. Since he was not well, most of his schooling was done at home while he was growing up.

As Roosevelt grew older, he finally gained his strength and became very busy. He loved to be outside in God's creation. He enjoyed hiking, fishing, and hunting. Roosevelt also enjoyed traveling around the world. He wrote books about what he saw on these trips as well.

Besides that, Roosevelt was busy in serving his country. He served as a soldier in the army and later became the President of the United States. Roosevelt wanted to be useful to God and to his country.

Roosevelt used all his strength to change his country for the better. He learned to make good use of his time on earth. While Theodore Roosevelt was president, he began many national parks. **National** means it belongs to all of the country. These special parks were set up so people would be able to see and enjoy

visiting some of the most beautiful forests and lakes that God created. Every year, millions of Americans enjoy visiting or camping in national parks. What parks have you visited?

Young Douglas MacArthur

Like most boys, Douglas MacArthur enjoyed pretending that he was an army soldier. This was easy for him to do because his dad was a soldier in the United States Army. Little Douglas loved to play with his toy gun and march around the kitchen table.

As Douglas grew up, his parents traveled from one part of the United States to another. When Douglas graduated from high school, his parents helped him get into the

Military Academy at West Point. Douglas spent four years at this military school and graduated at the top of his class.

After military school, MacArthur joined the army as an officer in charge of many soldiers. In 1917, he was sent to France to take part in a war in which many countries fought. It was called the **First World War**.

MacArthur was such a faithful leader that he was promoted to the rank of general during the war. One of his first jobs was to return to the Military Academy at West Point as its new leader. He made each student follow a set of rules called a "code of honor." This code said that students needed to live an honest and godly lifestyle.

General MacArthur Fights for Freedom

More than fifty years ago the world went to war again. So many nations in the world fought in this

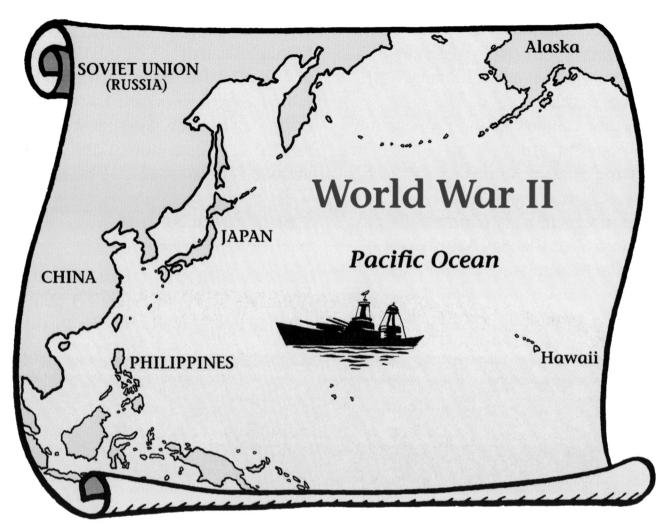

World War II

Pacific Ocean

SOVIET UNION (RUSSIA)

Alaska

JAPAN

CHINA

PHILIPPINES

Hawaii

war that it is called the **Second World War**. The leaders from Germany, Italy, and Japan joined together to steal land from other countries. The United States joined with England, Canada, France, the Soviet Union (now called Russia), and many other countries around the world to stop them. Can you find these countries on a globe?

On December 7, 1941, Japan attacked the United States. They dropped bombs on Pearl Harbor, which is in the state of Hawaii. Many soldiers and sailors died and many ships and planes were destroyed. Soon, the United States went to war against Japan. President Franklin Roosevelt asked General Douglas MacArthur to lead the United States

Army against the Japanese.

Since Japan stole land from many countries, General MacArthur had a lot of work to do. General MacArthur was able to help the United States Army take many island countries back from Japan. Then, he guided his soldiers to fight a battle to free the Philippines from Japan's control.

Finally, American boats called **submarines**, which can travel under water, sunk many ships from Japan. Planes dropped many bombs on the island nation. Since the homes in Japan were made of wood and paper, the cities and towns burned up fast. Many people were killed by the bombs. After many bombs were dropped and many ships were sunk, the people of Japan gave up fighting. General MacArthur helped make the world a safer place to live.

A submarine used in the Second World War

Words to Know

Repeat each of the following words as your teacher says them. Go back in your story to find these words and mark them with a highlighting marker.

invention   First World War

inventor   Second World War

national   submarines

Something to Do

Do you like to go to the library? If your mom or dad takes you there, you can choose a book about one of the following men: Theodore Roosevelt, George Washington Carver, Thomas Edison, or General MacArthur.

Or you may choose to do something with plants like George Washington Carver did many years ago. Take two paper or plastic cups and plant one seed in each cup. Be sure to put a little water in each cup every day. Put one cup near a window, and put the other cup in a closet. After many days, which plant grows better? Why? The one near the window grows better because of the sunlight. God gives us sunlight to grow plants.

Unit 13 Review

After you read each sentence, say the word that you think is missing. Write your answers on a separate sheet of paper.

1. American farmers were helped by George Washington _____.

2. The electric light bulb was invented by Thomas _____.

3. A new tool or machine that someone thinks about in his mind is called an _____.

4. The President who began many national parks was Theodore _____.

5. General Douglas _____ led the American army when it fought against the nation of Japan during World War II.

ANSWERS: 1. Carver 2. Edison 3. invention
4. Roosevelt 5. MacArthur

14 Exploring the United States

1. Washington, D.C.

Do you know what a **capital** city is? It is the city where the leaders of a country meet to pass laws and rule the people. If you can, you should

The Capitol Building

North America has many beautiful places that God has created for us to see and enjoy. Let us explore a few of the great places for "Little Pilgrims" to see in the United States. Many of them can also help us learn about history. Each part of America has interesting places to visit!

visit your country's capital city.

Washington, D. C., is the capital city of the United States. This city was built many years ago so America's leaders would have a place in which to meet. Every year, leaders from all

over the country come to Washington to make laws for the nation. This meeting is called **Congress** and it is held in the Capitol building. The following words are written on the walls inside the **dome** of the Capitol: "The New Testament according to the Lord and Savior Jesus Christ."

A group of people who work at the **Supreme Court** make sure that the laws that are made agree with the Constitution. They decide which laws in our nation are just and fair. You can visit the Supreme Court Building at certain times during the year. A **crier** begins each meeting of the court with the following words: "God save the United States and this Honorable Court."

The flag of the United States is

Places to Visit in North America
Match the number in the text with the place.

The Supreme Court

In the Bible we read, "Blessed is the nation whose God is the Lord" (Psalm 33:12a). This teaches that a nation can only be blessed if it follows the commands of the Lord Jesus Christ. Only those nations who honor Christ by believing on Him and obeying His laws can be truly great.

The top leader of the United States is called the President. He lives in a place called the **White House**. He should make sure that everything is working well in the government. He

often called the "Stars and Stripes." It has fifty stars on it, one star for each state in the nation and only thirteen stripes. When the country first began, the flag only had thirteen (13) stars and thirteen stripes on it. Do you know why the first United States flag had only thirteen stars and stripes?

The United States also has a great saying: "In God We Trust." An important sentence like this saying is called a **motto**. This motto is printed on our coins. Can you find the tiny letters where the motto is printed on some coins you have?

also asks Congress to make laws that will help the country. Do you know what laws they should follow when they think about making new laws? Yes, our leaders must make laws that agree with the Constitution and conform to the Bible.

The state that you live in also has a capital city. Do you know its name? Ask your teacher to help you find it on a map of your state.

Your state leaders meet in your capital to work on important laws. Maybe you can visit your state capital someday and meet some of the people who help make these laws.

2. Independence Hall in Philadelphia, Pennsylvania

The city of Philadelphia, Pennsylvania, is another interesting place to visit. Did you know that the word "Philadelphia" is found in the Bible? It means "brotherly love."

This city was very important in the early days of the United States. Many of the great leaders of our country, such as George Washington and Benjamin Franklin, used to visit Philadelphia often.

When the United States was freed from England, the people of Philadelphia rang a special bell in the center of town. This bell is known today as the "Liberty Bell." On it are written these words from the Bible: "...Proclaim liberty throughout all the land, unto all the inhabitants thereof" (Leviticus 25:10).

In 1787, a meeting was held in Independence Hall

The White House

Independence Hall

in Philadelphia. Many wise men came to write a plan for the new government. We learned that this plan is called the Constitution of the United States. The Constitution is the most important law in the land which everyone must obey. Do you remember who led this meeting? Yes, it was George Washington.

3. The Statue of Liberty in New York City

Another great sight to see is the Statue of Liberty. This tall bronze statue was given to the United States many years ago by the people of France. It sits on an island near the city of New York. You have to take a boat to visit it. The giant statue lets visitors know that our land holds out the light of freedom to people all

The Statue of Liberty

4. Boston, Massachusetts

Each year, many Americans like to visit the old city of Boston. This city was started in 1630 by a group of Christians from England we learned about before, called the Puritans. The Puritans also started the first college in the country. Harvard College was started to train pastors to preach the Word of God.

over the world. The poem at the bottom of the statue reads:

> "Give me your tired, your poor, Your huddled masses yearning to breathe free… Send these, the homeless, tempest-tost to me, I lift my lamp beside the golden door."

Faneuil Hall, the "Cradle of Liberty"

Boston is located in the state of Massachusetts. It is part of the area of our country that we call New England. The city of Boston has famous old churches and schools that you can visit. Boston also has many great museums and places to see from early American history. You may visit Faneuil Hall, which has been called the "Cradle of Liberty."

The *U.S.S. Constitution*

Many famous battles were also fought near Boston during the War for American Independence.

You can also visit an early American warship, the *U.S.S. Constitution* in Boston Harbor. It is fun to go on board this old ship and see the cannons and white sails.

5. The Alamo in San Antonio, Texas

Years ago, Texas was part of Mexico, which was ruled by Spain. Spain invited Americans to come and live in Texas. Soon most of the people in Texas were Americans. In the meantime, Mexico became free from Spain and wanted to have greater control over the Americans in Texas. The Americans, however, did not want Mexico to control them, so they decided to be free. General Santa Anna of Mexico led his army into Texas to defeat the Americans.

A group of brave men, including Col. James Bowie and Davy Crockett, joined together in the Alamo Mission. They prepared for battle. All of those men fought hard. In the end, however, they all died fighting for freedom.

The Alamo

When the Americans in Texas heard what happened to those brave men, they started to shout: "Remember the Alamo!" Men from all parts of Texas came to bravely defend their new country. General Sam Houston led the Texans to victory. Texas was now a free nation. General Houston was elected as its first president. Texas stayed an independent nation until 1845, when it joined the United States.

6. Rocky Mountain National Park in Colorado

North America is famous for its high Rocky Mountains in the west. Can you find them on a map? These mountains stretch from Alaska in the north, down through Canada, and into the United States.

The Rockies are called the "backbone of North America." Do you know what a backbone is? A **backbone** is the long line of bones

The Rockies in Colorado

down the middle of your back. On a map, the Rocky Mountains look like the backbone of a big, strong man.

Rocky Mountain National Park is in northern Colorado. The backbone called the Continental Divide runs through the park. It is filled with beautiful mountains, forests, and animals. If you go there, you should take warm clothing because it can be very cold any time during the year.

7. Yellowstone National Park in Wyoming

Many Americans go to the state of Wyoming each year to see the wonders of God's creation in Yellowstone National Park. It is the oldest national park in the world and the largest in the United States.

This park is known for its wild animals, mountains, and waterfalls. But this park is also known for its hot springs and geysers. A **hot spring** is a place where very hot water bubbles up from below the ground. A **geyser** is a hot spring which shoots out

Old Faithful

8. Mount Rushmore in South Dakota

Another great place to visit is Mount Rushmore in the Black Hills of South Dakota. Years ago, a group of artists made a big stone carving of the heads of four American presidents in the side of a mountain. How do you think they did it? They cut the faces of the presidents right out of the rock in the mountain!

Mount Rushmore is the largest stone carving in the world. Each year, thousands of Americans go to this hilly part of South Dakota to see the huge stone heads of Presidents Washington, Jefferson, Roosevelt, and Lincoln.

boiling water and steam straight into the air!

"Old Faithful" is the most famous geyser of all. It shoots off water and steam for five minutes every single hour. Steamboat Geyser is the largest geyser in Yellowstone; one time it shot water more than 400 feet into the air!

Words to Know

Repeat each of the following words as your teacher says them. Go back in your story to find these words and mark them with a highlighting marker.

Congress	White House
crier	Supreme Court
dome	capital
geyser	hot spring
backbone	

Something to Do

If you live near one of these great sights, plan to go and see it. If you live far from these places you could go to the library and find some picture books that tell all about them. Your library may have videos that show many of these sights as well.

Mount Rushmore

Unit 14 Review

After you read each sentence, say the word or words that you think are missing. Write your answers on a separate sheet of paper.

1. Congress is held in a building called the _____.

2. The capital city of the United States is _____, D.C.

3. The President of the United States lives in the _____ _____.

4. Each meeting of the Supreme Court is begun by a _____.

5. France gave the people of the United States the Statue of _____.

6. The city of Boston was started by the _____.

7. The largest stone carving in the world is called Mount _____.

ANSWERS: 1. Capitol 2. Washington
3. White House 4. prayer 5. Liberty
6. Puritans 7. Rushmore

15 Today and Tomorrow

Becoming a Servant of Christ

You can become a Christian servant. When you do, you will be a blessing to others. A **blessing** is the joy that comes when serving others for Christ. To be a blessing, you first need to trust and obey God. Then as you learn and grow, He will make you a blessing to others.

We are born with hearts full of sin. That is why people fight and why nations have wars. When you trust in Jesus, He will forgive your sins, clean your heart, and make you new inside. Then God will teach you His commands and how to be a servant.

How can you serve Jesus Christ today?

The first thing that you should do is to believe in Jesus Christ and trust Him to forgive your sins. You cannot serve God if your heart is dark with sin. God must clean your heart with the blood of Christ first.

When you know God, you will want to read His Word. Every day you should read part of the Bible to learn about God. You should want to go to church and worship God. Pay attention in Sunday School and try to understand the sermon. Then you will learn more about how you can love and serve God.

One important way to serve God is to give thanks for all He has given you. You can also pray for others. Pray for your father, mother, brothers, and sisters. Pray for your church and pray for your country and its leaders. Praying is one of the most important things you can do.

Today   Tomorrow   Return of Christ

God also tells you to keep His commandments. He tells you to turn from sin, do not fight with your brothers and sisters, do not lie or steal, be happy with what you have, and obey your parents. This is why you should memorize the Ten Commandments.

Another way to serve Christ is to study and work hard. Those who love the Lord Jesus work hard to please Him in all that they do. You should be eager to learn as you study your school books.

What do you want to do when you grow up?

God has given everyone different abilities. God wants you to serve Him with the talents He has given you.

Maybe you will be a fireman, lawyer, farmer, airline pilot, soldier, or an electrician. God alone knows what you should do with your life. Pray often and ask the Lord to lead you day by day. Learn the following verse by heart. It says the Lord will show you the way to go if you trust Him.

> Trust in the Lord with all thine heart; and lean not unto thine own understanding. In all thy ways acknowledge him, and he shall direct thy paths.
> —Proverbs 3:5-6

Many mothers work right in their own homes. Some train their children in the fear of the Lord and teach them at home. Others may work as teachers in a school or as a secretary in an office. Thank your parents for the jobs they do to help take care of you.

Families that follow Christ make strong churches, cities, and nations. Perhaps the most important job in

A Lawyer

A Farmer

A Pilot

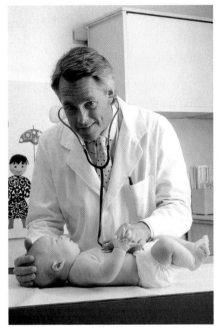

A Doctor

A Soldier

A Teacher

A Fireman

A Secretary

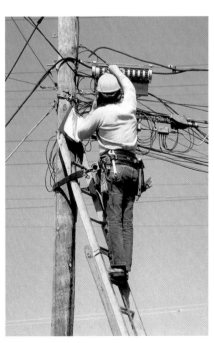

An Electrician

any nation is the work done by moms and dads. That is why the Bible says that they should train their children in the fear and discipline of Christ (Ephesians 6:4). Christian parents help raise their children to be the Christian servants of tomorrow.

The End of the Story

Just as every story has an ending, God's big story (His Story) also has an ending. At the very end of history, Jesus Christ will return to earth again. But this time He will not be born in a barn. No, he will come as the King of kings! When He comes, all people and all nations will bow before Him.

At the end of history, Christ will sit on His throne to judge everyone. If someone has believed in Jesus, he will enter into heaven. **Heaven** is a very happy place where God lives. In that day, a special book will be opened called the Book of Life. Everyone whose name is written in that book will be with Jesus forever. However, if someone has not believed in Jesus, he will go to hell. **Hell** is a very awful place where Satan will be. Everyone whose name is not in the Book of Life will be thrown into a lake of fire that burns forever.

People have done many good things and many bad things in history. We have studied some of them. When Jesus Christ returns He will tell everyone what was good and what was bad. He is the **Judge**.

When Christ is done judging, every knee shall bow before Him and every tongue shall say, "Jesus is Lord." Then, everyone that ever lived in this long story of history will know that Jesus is King! God began history when He created the world. God will end history when Christ returns.

What did you learn?

Before we end our study of world and American history, it is important to remember what we have learned. One more time, we will quickly go over God's Story—His Story—to help you remember.

Our study began with the true story about God making the first man and woman in the Garden of Eden. But when Adam and Eve fell into sin, God punished them. We then learned how the Lord made the different nations by making people to move away from each other.

We also heard about the great promise that God first gave to Abraham, Isaac, and Jacob, who then started the nation of Israel. He promised to send a Savior that would bring His people out of sin. God was with the people of Israel while He made the other nations ready to hear the good news about the Promised One, Jesus.

Finally God sent the Savior Jesus Christ into the world. *Jesus died on the cross and was raised from the dead to bring new life.* This was the most important thing that happened in history.

Then the apostles brought the good news about Jesus to a lot of other places. Many churches were started in the Roman Empire, but people suffered and died for

following Christ. Then we learned about how some of these churches became weak. We saw how false teachers came into the church so it did not follow the Bible any more.

But God loved His people and sent godly men to lead them back to the Bible. He sent the Reformers to preach the good news and to explain the Bible. Then the Lord gave many good things to the nations who followed His Word.

After that, we learned about the people who began to explore the continents of North and South America. Brave explorers like Columbus sailed far across the Atlantic Ocean and many people followed. Then new colonies were set up in the Americas by people from Spain, England, Holland, and France.

The English colonies became stronger as the years passed. God brought a Great Awakening to turn their hearts to Him. Leaders from the thirteen English colonies then decided to start their own country.

After the Americans fought hard for their freedom from England, the United States of America became a new nation. Slowly the country grew as settlers moved west across North America. The small country of thirteen states grew into a strong nation of fifty states.

We hope you have learned many new things in your trip through history. May Almighty God use these teachings to prepare you to be a servant of Christ. When you follow Christ, you will become God's "Little Pilgrim."

Words to Know

Repeat each of the following words as your teacher says them. Go back in your story to find these words and mark them with a highlighting marker.

blessing   heaven

hell   judge

Something to Do

Pretend that you are all grown up and you want to be a farmer, doctor, nurse, missionary, pastor, teacher, or a mother that stays at home to train and teach her children according to God's Word.

If your parents have some old clothes, maybe they would let you dress up just like they do. Or, if you have some toys—such as a doctor's kit or a tool box—you could pretend you are a doctor or carpenter.

Memorize Rev. 22:20. This Bible verse is very important. It teaches that Christ is going to return to the earth one day. Stop and learn this verse by heart.

Unit 15 Review

After you read each sentence, say the word that you think is missing. Write your answers on a separate sheet of paper.

1. "Blessed is the nation whose God is the _____."

2. You need to trust in Jesus Christ to become a _____.

3. Strong churches, cities, and nations are made by strong _____.

4. One of the most important things that you can do for your family, church, and country is to _____.

5. The Judge who will tell everyone what was good and what was bad is _____ _____.

6. When you follow Christ, you will become God's "Little _____."

ANSWERS: 1. Lord 2. Christian 3. families
4. pray 5. Jesus Christ 6. Pilgrim

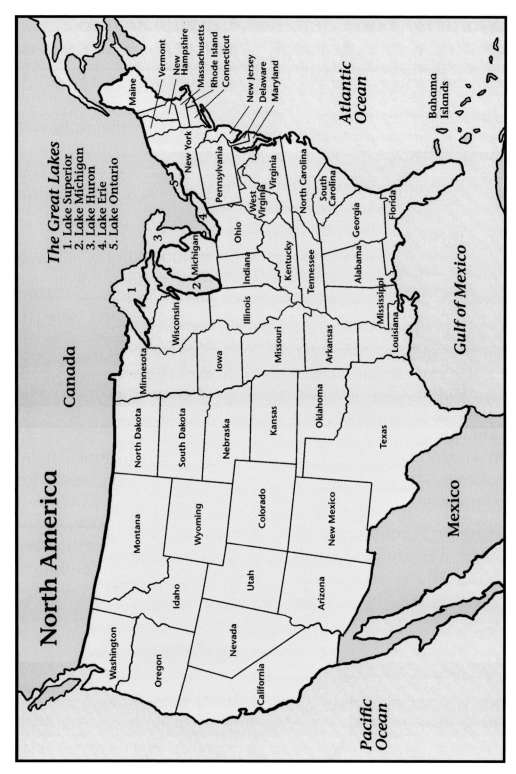

North America

Canada

The Great Lakes
1. Lake Superior
2. Lake Michigan
3. Lake Huron
4. Lake Erie
5. Lake Ontario

Vermont
New Hampshire
Massachusetts
Rhode Island
Connecticut
New Jersey
Delaware
Maryland

Maine
New York
Pennsylvania
West Virginia
Virginia
North Carolina
South Carolina
Georgia
Florida

Michigan
Wisconsin
Minnesota
Ohio
Indiana
Illinois
Iowa
Kentucky
Tennessee
Missouri
Arkansas
Alabama
Mississippi
Louisiana

North Dakota
South Dakota
Nebraska
Kansas
Oklahoma
Texas

Montana
Wyoming
Colorado
New Mexico

Washington
Oregon
Idaho
Nevada
Utah
Arizona
California

Mexico

Atlantic Ocean

Bahama Islands

Gulf of Mexico

Pacific Ocean